T0171513

Warnings of a Watchman

Thomas D. Logie

Order this book online at www.trafford.com
or email orders@trafford.com

Most Trafford titles are also available at major online book retailers.

Printed in Victoria, BC, Canada.

ISBN: 978-1-4269-2771-3 (sc)

ISBN: 978-1-4269-2772-0 (e-book)

*Our mission is to efficiently provide the world's finest, most comprehensive
book publishing service, enabling every author to experience success.
To find out how to publish your book, your way, and have it available
worldwide, visit us online at www.trafford.com*

Trafford rev. 3/30/2010

North America & international
toll-free: 1 888 232 4444 (USA & Canada)
phone: 250 383 6864 ♦ fax: 812 355 4082

FOREWARD

In the title I speak of a "watchman," taken from Ezekiel 3 and Ezekiel 33. In the ancient world, the watchman was a sentry in a tower searching alertly for trouble within his line of sight. In good weather with flat terrain he could have seen many miles even with the naked eye. It was his duty to sound a timely warning so that the people could take refuge and prepare for defense in case of a raid or invasion. In more modern warfare skirmishers or scouts serve this function for an organized military force.

In social and political affairs today, our news media are supposed to sound initial warnings of trouble to come. A newscaster covering an earthquake such as the recent one in Haiti cannot gloss over the misery present. Neither can I suppress what I know of the trouble ahead even though the portion of the truth that I see is alarming and occasionally gruesome.

Funny I am not. My friends might kid me that I barely know the difference between the humerus bone and a humorous joke. But since the subjects on my heart are serious, I should at least try to take a somewhat lighter tone for an introduction. So I am borrowing a device from David Letterman, with whom I would seldom agree. It is a fairly debatable subject whether I have hit all of the top ten reasons and certainly their order is subject to debate as well. I have used experience instead of polling data to compose these. However, I believe that all ten of these reasons can be substantiated from Scripture even though I may have missed others. If you are already a believer, think of this as an appetizer for the spiritual meal yet to come.

TOP TEN REASONS WHY PEOPLE REFUSE JESUS' OFFER OF EVERLASTING LIFE

10. Many people would rather be rich in money or "stuff" than rich in faith toward God.

The Lord Jesus addressed this in his parable of the farmer whose bumper crops were so large that he decided to build larger barns to replace his outdated ones and then stop working. Luke 12: 16-21. In verse 20 Jesus quotes God as saying to the wealthy farmer, *You fool, this night your soul shall be required of you: then whose shall those things be, which you have provided?* We feel secure with a large portfolio of assets, but we are not truly secure at all for that reason. The rich man and the beggar Lazarus both died about the same time (Luke 16:19-31).

The Bible does not tell us the ultimate fate of the rich young ruler (Matthew 19:16-26; Mark 10:17-27). He apparently was a moral young man who perceived enough of the Lordship of Jesus Christ to kneel before Him. He had avoided youthful excess. When the Biblical account ends, the young man was sad, wanting the follow Christ but cling to his riches at the same time when Jesus commanded otherwise. If this young man fell short of the kingdom of heaven, it was because he clung to his wealth in preference to Jesus Christ.

If any has wealth, he or she is responsible to God for how he or she uses it. Lavish people such as the various women of "Real Housewives" spend plenty of money but never achieve peace. Christians who have extra money often give much of it away; they would be uncomfortable spending it on wild parties and similar expenses. Wealth is not itself sinful, but the greedy consumption of things we don't need is sinful.

People also know that Christianity does not permit dishonest methods of gaining wealth even if the methods are successful. If monetary wealth is one's primary goal in life, Christianity will get in the way. Our primary goal is to "serve God and to enjoy Him forever" in the words of the old Westminster Confession. Wealth may or may not be a byproduct of such a life, but faith and peace will flow from such a life.

9. They would rather be with their friends, and their friends will be in Hell (more accurately, the Lake of Fire, but I will use the common concept here).

Will these people still be their friends when that time comes? How will anyone continue to enjoy friendship amid the crying, screams, curses and shrieks of pain in total darkness? Do you think you can have a dance, a sporting event, a poker game or even a decent conversation there? How will anyone even recognize relatives in the superheated, sulfurous and pitch-dark Lake of Fire? Even a concentration camp or the Black Hole of Calcutta does not give a true illustration of the horrors of the Lake of Fire. Friendship will not survive.

People are familiar and comfortable with their friends and are fearful to break away from them. To worship Jesus Christ today takes some courage, and it appears that in the future it will require much more courage than it does now. In some countries today, one may be threatened with death for the worship of Jesus Christ, as were many Christians under Roman rule before Constantine. In some cases knowing Christ enriches family contact, but in others professing Him means turning one's back on family and friends. As Matthew 19:29 says, *And every one that has forsaken houses, or brethren, or sisters, or father, or mother, or wife, or children, or lands, for My name's sake, shall receive an hundredfold, and shall inherit everlasting life.*

Fear of the reactions of family and friends is a factor in holding people back from calling on Jesus Christ to save and change them, but this is no excuse. Look at the converts who do call on the Lord Jesus even though they know full well that their own families will try to kill them. The recent case of the 17-year-old from Ohio who fled her family for Florida is an example in the United States, but such struggles occur daily in countries like Pakistan and Iran. There are thousands in various countries who risk jobs or even life for Jesus Christ. Thankfully, love for

Jesus Christ because of His saving work will overcome fear. *Perfect love casts out fear.* 1 John 4:18

8. Heaven will be sooooooooooooooooo boring.

People who think this may have a point in their present state of mind. Take music for an example. I don't think that one will hear in heaven any music that is Top 40 with any age group. Most of the popular music of my generation still had melody but also had an evil message. Gary Puckett of the Union Gap sang "Lady Willpower," a song about a man persuading a girl to sacrifice her virginity. Jose Feliciano was acclaimed for the explicitly raunchy song "Light My Fire." Another popular immoral tune ran "If You're Not With the One You Love, Love the One You're With." Frank Sinatra was of an older generation but "I Did It My Way." Then consider how several top musicians who sang of depression became suicides. Kurt Cobain was one. To most people today what we know of heaven and the perpetual worship of Jesus Christ strikes no note of joy or even hope. People who think this way are right in sensing that in their present state of mind they would not enjoy heavenly music nor anything about heaven. So many things (not only music, but athletics and other forms of entertainment, among other things) that we enjoy on earth will be superseded and forgotten in heaven. Because so many people do not know Him, they have no clue of what they will be missing or of what they will be suffering.

7. The same names that people have cursed on earth ("Oh God" or "Jeeeeeesus", for example) will have the highest and most praised names and places in heaven.

If someone is of a state of mind to take the names of God in vain and use them as curses, will that person enjoy hearing those names celebrated and exalted forever without end? If someone on earth finds the Bible boring or even offensive, will that person enjoy finding the Bible forever settled in heaven? The names of God are themselves sacred and are to be used only with reverence and respect and of God, Jesus and the Holy Spirit alone. This is the core of the Third Commandment.

Permit me an appeal to your common sense. If you knew that a particular judge were going to sentence you for an offense, you would ask your attorney questions about that judge to learn more about him or her. You would also be very careful to express only respect for that judge and for that court. Jesus Christ will judge everyone; why are so many (perhaps you?) using His name or the name of His Father as a curse when He will be fully aware of the curses when He judges each person?

6. God is a jealous God Who demands exclusive and everlasting loyalty to Himself.

The present culture discourages permanent relationships, even in marriage. For most modern people, relationships survive or die according to what they do for us. With God, relationships do not depend on momentary satisfaction but on laws and principles dictated by God Himself that do not change with circumstances (with relationships between human beings, there are certain exceptions that may break relationships that are likewise laid out by God and not by ourselves, but a proper relationship with God Himself will never be broken).

The jealousy of God is expressed in the First Commandment in Exodus 20:3: *You shall have no other gods before Me.* This principle is equally true of possessions, as we have already perceived from the example of the rich young ruler. Jesus said during his discussion of wealth in the Sermon on the Mount (Matthew 6:19-34 with verse 24 quoted here), *No man can serve two masters: for either he will hate the one, and love the other; or else he will hold to the one, and despise the other. You cannot serve God and mammon.*

5. The way toward heaven is a demanding and difficult path (Matthew 7:13-14). Most people would rather take the path of least resistance and think about the consequences later or simply ignore them.

The Lord Jesus does not allow anyone into heaven through surface repairs of the sinful human nature with which we are born. He demands a complete change of the inner man, which starts with the new birth and which will be finished when we finally reach His presence. Most people naturally resist the change because they have no clue as to the end of their road.

For example, no sensible person would undergo radiation treatment if healthy. But if one discovers a serious cancer, radiation might be considered seriously despite its awful side effects. In Jeremiah 31 and Ezekiel 36, God prescribes a heart-lung transplant because we have sinful hearts and spirits which will lead us to everlasting death. Yet most of us are convinced that we are healthy and therefore refuse the prescribed treatment because it is viewed as pointless pain.

4. The way of the world is self-assertion; the way to heaven involves self-denial.

"I gotta be me" goes the Frank Sinatra song. There is just enough truth in this lyric to make it dangerous. In truth I need to enter economic pursuits for which I am suited. I would be a fool to try to be a professional athlete or a professional dancer. Through the grace of God I have been able to help some people as a lawyer. But when dealing with God Himself, the lyric is all wrong. If I remain like myself, I become more and more offensive to Him. Instead I need to become less like my natural self and more like His Son Jesus Christ. This involves self-denial and the progressive substitution of character traits like the Lord Jesus and unlike my original nature. Modern pop psychology and even some the titles of modern books written by contemporary pastors (for example, <u>Be a Better You</u>) try to turn Christian discipleship upside down or at least dilute it so much that it loses its power. We do not need merely to be a better or more efficient self -- we need to be a better and more efficient Christian. Peter and Paul did not become better versions of their natural selves -- they became totally different people through Jesus Christ. Peter and Paul could not conform to the demands of Nero; neither can the modern Christian conform to the demands of modern culture.

3. Some people are so bull-headed that they do not want to listen to anybody -- even God. At bottom this reflects pride.

There is an old saying, "I'd rather do it myself." Sometimes in earthly matters this attitude will protect us from fraudsters, but in spiritual matters we must acknowledge and confess our sin and our lack of knowledge when compared to God. Pride has historically been known as one of the seven deadly sins and is one of the things that God hates. Proverbs 6:16-19; 8:13, 11:2, 16:18-19, and 29:23 are examples.

1 John 2:16 classifies sin under three headings: the lust of the flesh, the lust of the eyes and the pride of life. This reason most directly aims at the pride of life. The lusts of the flesh and eyes are addressed in various other of these "Top Ten."

2. People hate Jesus Christ because He brings their sins into the open.

John the Apostle introduces the Lord Jesus as the Word of God and then as the Light of the World. John 1:4-9. One characteristic of natural light is that it exposes hidden things. All kinds of morally corrupt sins done or spoken behind closed doors will be exposed on Judgment Day. In politics, we speak of metaphorical sunshine as a way of limiting secret, corrupt deals in government. John 3:19-20 says this:

And this is the condemnation, that light is come into the world, and men loved darkness rather than light, because their deeds were evil. For every one that does evil hates the light, neither comes to the light, lest his deeds should be reproved.

Imagine for a moment that you were in Laon, France in May 1940 just sitting down to supper when the radio broadcast the news that the German Army was 10 miles away and headed right at you. Your first reaction with your neighbors would be to close up the house and scramble away by any means possible. There's no time to eat supper or even clean up if you are going to get away. In fact such scenes were played out throughout northeast France.

Suppose someone looked into your abandoned house 10 days later, with the food still on the table. The house has been dark the entire time. What would you guess would be populating the kitchen and dining room? And what would be their reaction when someone shined a flashlight into the rooms? Naturally, we would think that a variety of repulsive creatures would run for cover from the light. When Jesus Christ shines the searchlight of the Holy Scriptures on the dark recesses of our soul, we have the same initial reaction -- to run for any cover available.

If running away from Him to keep "doing our own thing" in spiritual darkness is our "Final Answer," we are doomed and damned. No wonder that some people hate Jesus Christ!

If you love Jesus Christ instead of hating Him, the basic idea of revealing dark secrets still applies to our lives. Consider 1 Corinthians 4:5:

> *Therefore judge nothing before the time, until the Lord come, who both will bring to light the hidden things of darkness, and will make manifest the counsels of the hearts: and then shall every man have praise of God.*

1. People hate Jesus Christ because He demands holiness in all aspects of our lives.

Our Lord Jesus was introduced to Israel and to the world by John the Baptist, the last and greatest of the prophets. Luke 3:1-14 summarizes the message of John the Baptist. He told everyone to repent of their sins, calling them "vipers" and asking them "*Who warned you to flee from the wrath to come?*" He warned those with power not to abuse it by collecting extra taxes or by bullying people. He told people who had extra to share it. John's public ministry was halted when he was arrested for denouncing the sexual immorality of a governor for marrying his brother's wife. Luke 3:18-20; Matthew 14:1-11; Mark 6:14-28. For this John was executed through the anger of that unlawful wife and the lust in the governor that was incited by suggestive dancing. That governor well knew that he was violating justice but ordered the execution notwithstanding his qualms of conscience.

Pilate similarly knew that Jesus was guiltless (*"I find no fault"* is a finding of "not guilty.") but nevertheless ordered Him crucified to appease the crowd and in repayment for the pledge of the contemporary Jewish leadership that they *"had no king but Caesar."* (John 19:4-16, quoting directly from verse 15. The leadership had repudiated God as King also. The leadership and Pilate united in an unholy bargain at Jesus' expense. Little did either side know how God's good purposes would be accomplished by their evil intent, as with Jacob's son Joseph, on a vastly greater scale.) Like His forerunner John the Baptist, the Lord Jesus commands *"all men everywhere to repent."* (quoting from Paul's sermon to the intellectuals of Athens in Acts 17:30). People did not like it then and do not like it now.

If you read carefully the entire Sermon on the Mount (Matthew 5-7), you will see how hopeless it is to try to live a pure, holy life through self-effort. Except for Jesus Christ, none can observe this fully -- but this summarizes what Jesus Christ demands of all of us. *Except you repent, you will all likewise perish.* Luke 13:3, repeated by the Lord Jesus in Luke 13:5. So Jesus remains hated today as He was hated when He lived in His human body on earth.

But such hatred is an eternally fatal error which will make certain that a human being will experience forever the "wrath to come" of which John the Baptist warned. The ancient message of hope given by Paul in his public sermon at Antioch in Pisidia is still open to anyone today:

For David, after he had served his own generation by the will of God, fell on sleep [i.e. died], and was laid unto his fathers, and saw corruption: But He [Jesus], whom God raised again, saw no corruption. Be it known unto you therefore, men and brethren, that through this Man is preached unto you the forgiveness of sins. And by Him all that believe are justified from all things, from which you could not be justified by the law of Moses. Beware therefore, lest that come upon you, which is spoken of in the prophets; "Behold, ye despisers, and wonder, and perish: for I work a work in your days, a work which you shall in no wise believe, though a man declare it to you." [quoting Habakkuk 1:5 given originally in the context of the Babylonian conquest of Judah] Acts 13:36-41.

So repentance and faith in the risen Lord Jesus Christ are the start of eternal life in the place of eternal punishment. Repent and believe!

Introduction

I will be saying some hard, unpleasant things about humanity in general. Some of them may apply to you. They apply as much to me as to anyone else. I, too, was born spiritually dead and a sinner by nature and choice. I deserved the perpetual rejection and anger of God. I have been changed by His mercy. They was nothing about me that should have moved Him to mercy, but He chose to do so for reasons originating in Himself and not in me. As Paul said, *In me, that is in my flesh, dwells no good thing.* Romans 7:18. I have been given a privilege of sharing pieces of divine truth even though I am imperfect. I should also mention that I am trusting the discretion of the reader to determine how mature a person should be when subjects are introduced and discussed. I would recommend than an adult read this book before determining how much of it would be appropriate for a child. I realize that children are exposed quickly to sensitive subjects in the 21st century, so some parents will opt to use more of this book earlier as a counteraction to the sexualized and ungodly culture in which we live (in the U.S.A.).

While I desire to witness to the world and to advise my children and other posterity especially concerning family, there is an introductory subject that I have to approach before I can discuss family relationships given modern culture. As I write in early 2010, the majority of intellectual leaders at least profess to believe that humanity is the highest form of intelligence on earth and may well be the highest form of intelligence in the entire universe. This is why so many intelligent intellectuals fight so stubbornly for macro-evolution -- the belief that humanity evolved from less intelligent and complex forms of animal life. The real issue is not the scientific evidence but rather the insistence of the majority of modern humanity that humanity -- whether the individual man or woman as in the case of Ayn Rand or the collective in the case of modern dictators both left and right -- is the highest and greatest authority. A dictator with a "cult of personality" (the phrase of Nikita Khrushchev of the former USSR, a participant, witness and survivor of Stalin's violence, who surely was an authority on the "cult of personality" from experience) will naturally cultivate a doctrine of humanity as the highest authority. That idea deprives dissidents of the leverage of a higher authority to which dissidents can appeal. Indeed, dissidents through the centuries such as Jeremiah the prophet, Luther in Reformation Germany, Wycliffe in late 14th-century England, Tyndale in the time of Henry VIII in the 1530s, Solzhenitsyn in the 20th-century USSR, Watchman Nee in 20th-century Red China and Bonhoeffer in Nazi Germany have appealed to God and to the Scriptures (or the portions then written) to challenge dictators. Martin Luther King quoted Scripture to challenge segregation in the southern portion of the United States. While I would not endorse every theological or political position that each of these dissenters took (except that Jeremiah wrote 2 books of Holy Scriptures which are beyond reproach), these men did find a place to stand against both dictators and oppressive majorities in the Scriptures. Dictators as a rule will not listen to or even tolerate dissent on earth. Before you can have any structure to your life, you have to settle in your mind and heart the issue of the ultimate authority in your life. I can assure you from history that anyone who thinks that he or she is the highest authority in his or her own life is headed for trouble. Similarly, anyone who selects another fallible human being as the highest and final authority over his or her own life will find themselves in lasting trouble in short order. For an extended historical example of one person who did this, read Albert Speer's autobiography written in prison after he had served as Hitler's architect and then as Minister of Armaments in Nazi Germany.

It is fashionable today to disparage the Bible. Such disparagement is contrary to America's historical roots, even among our forefathers who did not believe in an evangelical faith. For example, at the Jefferson Memorial there is the inscription from his own writings: "I tremble for my nation when I remember that God is just." Jefferson for most and perhaps all of his life did not believe in the deity of Jesus Christ nor in His miracles, but at least he recognized a just God who intervenes in the rise and fall of nations. Benjamin Franklin, another Founding Father, insisted that the delegates to the

Constitutional Convention pray daily before their deliberations. George Washington was more definitely a Christian in his beliefs. Roger Sherman of Connecticut and John Jay, the first chief Justice of the United States Supreme Court, were known as devout Christians in their own time. It is true that Thomas Paine, the author of the 1776 pamphlet <u>Common Sense</u>, did not believe in God's existence, but he was the rare exception. In fact he left the United States for revolutionary France and did not return here until Napoleon had risen to power in France, most likely because there was too much faith in the United States for him to be comfortable. But it should also be noted that the government of the United States with its strong Christian and Biblical influence was far more stable and less bloody than the various governments in revolutionary and atheistic France between the fall of the monarchy (started in 1789 and completed in 1792) and the rise of Napoleon near 1800. Napoleon ended the disorder with another dictatorship, although it should be granted that Napoleon allowed citizens more rights than the absolute monarchies and the revolutionary governments that preceded him.

To summarize the lessons of ancient and modern human history, mankind cannot govern itself. As William Pitt, a great English Prime Minister said, "The nation that will not be governed by God will be governed by tyrants!" Winston Churchill and Margaret Thatcher would have agreed. Human government is a necessity because of our sin. Romans 13:1-7; 1 Peter 2:13-116.

The Holy Scriptures are binding, authoritative and were sent and breathed by God (the literal translation of "inspiration" in 2 Timothy 3:16: *All scripture is given by inspiration of God, and is profitable for doctrine, for reproof, for correction, for instruction in righteousness.*) We are solemnly warned against adding or subtracting from them. *Do not add to His words, lest He reprove you and you be found a liar.* Proverbs 30:6. *To the law and to the testimony: if they speak not according to this word, it is because there is no light in them.* Isaiah 8:20. *For I [Jesus in His resurrected state -- see Revelation 22:16 to confirm this] testify unto every man that hears the words of the prophecy of this book, if any man shall add unto these things, God shall add unto him the plagues that are written in this book. And if any man shall take away from the words of the book of this prophecy, God shall take away his part out of the book of life, and out of the holy city, and from the things which are written in this book.* Revelation 22:18-19. While each teacher including myself will be imperfect, we must take care not to pollute the source of truth by passing passing off our own understanding as itself Scripture. No religious authority has any authority to add or amend the teachings of the Scriptures as a whole. I must transmit and amplify them with as little distortion as possible. We all must obey the Scriptures. I seek to follow the teachers of Nehemiah 8:8: *So they read in the book in the law of God distinctly, and gave the sense, and caused them to understand the reading.* In fact, I and every other teacher of the Bible will face a stricter standard of judgment because we are handling the Holy Scriptures as distinct from mathematics, science, literature or other human learning. James 3:1.

The Holy Scriptures give us a better way. We have to start by acknowledging that we cannot govern ourselves as individuals any more than a nation can function without some form of government. As Jeremiah said (10:23), *"O LORD, I know that the way of man is not in himself: it is not in man that walks to direct his steps. O LORD, correct me, but with judgment; not in Your anger, lest You bring me to nothing."* Acknowledging God as sovereign over us gives up any claim that we are autonomous, but it also gives us a compass to guide us through life. We do not have to walk alone, whether married or single. I can state from experience that some of the loneliest times that one may face may be in marriage when you and your mate are in basic disagreement. Marriage by itself is not a guarantee of real companionship. Only God Himself is fully dependable as a companion. Our Lord Jesus promised, *I will never leave you nor forsake you.* Hebrews 13:5.

God's sovereignty is not just an abstract concept; it has concrete meaning in our lives. Consider Psalm 24:1-2. *The earth is the Lord's and the fullness of it; the world, and they that dwell in it. For He has founded it upon the seas and established it upon the floods.* We have already mentioned the concept that human beings belong to God. This passage reaffirms that and adds that the earth itself belongs to God. So if we own real estate, our title is only good against other human beings like ourselves. God is still the ultimate owner. In terms of raw power, we are helpless if He chooses to send a disaster such as a tornado or a tsunami against our house. Isaiah 45:7 says that *I form the light, and create darkness: I make peace, and create evil (calamity): I the LORD do all these things.*

Our Lord Jesus commended the wisdom of a king who would consider making peace if his army were to be outnumbered 2 to 1. Luke 14:31-32. Likewise I advise you to make peace with Jesus Christ by surrendering to Him immediately. In terms of power you cannot fight Him for even an instant if He chooses to concentrate His force against you. You and I live at all only because of His longsuffering patience.

This truth is amplified in many other Scriptures. Psalm 65:6-7 reminds us that God set the boundaries of both natural bodies of water and of nations. For other aspects of this basic idea review Jeremiah 5:22 and Psalms 29:10, 74:15-17, 89:9, 93:3-4 and 107:25-29. The Lord Jesus even demonstrated his sovereignty over the elements by walking on water and by stopping the wind with one sentence: *Peace, be still!* Matthew 14:25; Mark 4:39. For further reinforcement of this concept, consider Job 38-41 and Psalm 148:7-10.

Are earthquakes under the control of God? Indeed they are. They are also harbingers of the judgment to come. Perhaps this is why earthquakes give so many people the shakes (the pun is intended). They cannot be controlled by humanity; we are reminded of our helplessness. One earthquake interrupted the 1989 World Series for a week. Haggai 2:6-7 says this, *For thus says the Lord of Hosts, "Yet once a little while, and I will shake the heavens, the earth, the sea and the dry land. And I will shake all nations, and the Desire of Nations shall come, and I will fill this house with glory.* Isaiah 24 as a whole deals with the Last Judgment and verses 19-20 probably refer to the same last earthquake described by Haggai: *The earth is utterly broken down; the earth is clean dissolved. The earth is moved exceedingly. The earth shall reel to and fro like a drunkard and shall be removed like a cottage. The transgression of it shall be heavy on it. It shall fall and not rise again.* The preliminary earthquakes that we may experience now (literally called "birthpangs" in Matthew 24:8) are leading up to that last great quake. Like physical childbirth, they are gradually becoming more frequent and will become more intense. This earth is figuratively pregnant with a new, perfect and untainted earth.

The Scriptures tell us that God controls all the basic necessities of life. All human beings need food to survive. In this present world, we adults have to work for our food -- our children must gradually learn how to work to earn food for themselves. *If anyone will not work, neither shall he eat.* 2 Thessalonians 3:10. But we still need God's permission for our labors to succeed in bringing in food or something that can be exchanged for food. And so we must pray to God as Jesus taught in His most familiar prayer, *Give us this day our daily bread [ration].* This was not new with the Lord Jesus. Consider Psalm 28:9: *Save Your people, and bless your inheritance; feed them also, and lift them up forever.* (While this verse can apply to food for the soul as well as for the body, for clarity I will stick to the most basic physical meaning for now.) Proverbs 30:8-9 agrees: *Remove far from me vanity and lies. Give me neither poverty nor riches. Feed me with food suitable for me, lest I be full and deny You and say "Who is the Lord?" Or lest I be poor and steal and take the name of my God in vain.* While work is the usual means for God to provide us food, it is not the only way. Elijah in 1 Kings 17 was fed by ravens and then from the bottom of two containers that did not run out for years. Our Lord Jesus fed 5000 men and their families on one occasion and 4000 men and their families on another occasion with only one person's meal as a start. In both cases there were leftovers. In the Wilderness several million children of Israel were fed directly from heaven for approximately 40 years. God can use miracles to feed His people when he chooses to do so.

Who provides our clothing? God! Consider another portion of the Lord Jesus' Sermon on the Mount: *And why do you take thought for clothing? Behold the lilies of the field, how they grow. They do not toil; neither do they spin. Yet I say to you that Solomon in all his glory was not clothed like one of these. Therefore if God so clothes the grass of the field, which today exists and tomorrow is thrown into the oven, shall He not much more clothe you, O you of little faith?* Matthew 6:28-30.

These passages are important for the specific natural occurrences which they teach are under God's control, but the most important idea is found in their combination -- that God is in control of all of nature. Even the skeptic Thomas Jefferson recognized the sovereignty of "nature's God" in the Declaration of Independence. Jesus Christ demonstrated his Deity in part by demonstrating His control over nature.

Therefore, one ground of why God has the right to command and instruct us about family life is based on His authority and knowledge as the Creator and His exertion of that power that we call gravity that holds things together. Colossians 1:16-17. This is a sufficient basis in itself for the universal obligation of all human beings to obey Him on family and other matters.

For anyone who claims to believe in God, there is a second and even greater reason: if your profession is true, then you have been purchased from being a slave to sin and have been set free from the power of sin. Our Lord Jesus states this clearly in John 8:31-36:

> *Then said Jesus to those Jews which believed on him, If you continue in My word, then are you My disciples indeed; And you shall know the truth, and the truth shall make you free.*
>
> *They answered him, We are Abraham's seed, and were never in bondage to any man: how do you say, You shall be made free?*
>
> *Jesus answered them, Truly, truly, I say unto you, Whosoever commits sin is the servant (literally: slave) of sin. And the servant (slave) does not abide in the house for ever: but the Son abides ever. If the Son therefore shall make you free, you shall be free indeed.*

Since except for Jesus Himself every human being commits sin, we all start as slaves of sin unless and until the Son -- Jesus Christ -- has set us free. Our Lord Jesus stated later, "*I am the Way, the Truth and the Life; no man comes to the Father except through Me.*" John 14:6. The truth that sets free in John 8 has intellectual content but is not merely intellectual. For a quick version of the intellectual kernel dealing with the death and resurrection of Jesus Christ, read 1 Corinthians 15:3-8. Jesus Christ is the epitome of truth -- the Truth. So to be set free we need to know intellectual truth but most of all the personal resurrected Living Truth, Jesus Christ.

The Apostle Paul confirms this in Romans 8:2, *For*

the law of the Spirit of life in Christ Jesus has made me free from the law of sin and death. In Ephesians 2:1 this same idea is expressed in terms of spiritual life and death, *And you has He made alive, who were dead in trespasses and sins.* The Way to life and freedom is Christ Jesus. In family matters specifically, He shows the way to life and peace. But before we pursue that, I should explain in more detail how the believer has been bought by Christ Jesus.

We have already seen our original slavery to sin at birth. Certainly the passage in Ephesians 2 shows that we cannot escape our shackles in our own power. On our own, we would not want to escape. Consider Ephesians 2:3, which says, *Among whom [the children of disobedience in context from v. 2] also we all had our behavior in times past in the lusts of our flesh, fulfilling the desires of the flesh and of the mind; and were by nature the children of wrath, even as others.* The prophet Jeremiah spoke similarly centuries earlier: *Can the Ethiopian change his skin, or the leopard his spots? then may you also do good, that are accustomed to do evil.* Jeremiah 13:23. Before anyone hits a panic button, Jeremiah was not a racist. The passage does **not** teach that the color of the Ethiopian's skin is better or worse than any other hue, but only that it cannot be changed by human effort any more than a leopard can change its spots by its effort. (People through the ages have changed their hair color, but skin color is impossible to change for any sustained period of time.) The people who are denounced in this passage are Jeremiah's contemporaries in Judah, who prided themselves on being God's people without the change of heart that God requires for fellowship with Him. While skin color makes no spiritual difference whatsoever, the skin of the targets of Jeremiah's "calling out" was of olive complexion as a matter of historical fact. The point is that Jeremiah centuries before Christ pointed out the helplessness of sinful man to change his own evil nature. In fact, Jeremiah (chapters 30-33) and Ezekiel (chapter 36) both testify to the necessity of a heart-lung transplant -- to replace the evil heart and spirit of a person with a new one. (The word "spirit" in Hebrew has a double meaning which includes breath also.) Plainly we cannot do this for ourselves in the natural world. Neither can we do it in the spiritual world. Someone else must do it for us.

This is the point where the ransom of Jesus Christ (Matthew 20:28) enters the picture. The justice of God requires that the truth of our offensiveness to God be faced squarely. There is no such thing as a "free pass." So Jesus, the perfect and sinless Son of God, undertook to pay the penalty for the sin of every believer so that God would change rather than destroy those believers (including me) as we all deserve to be destroyed perpetually. Under the Law of Moses a Passover Lamb was killed as a temporary sacrifice before Jesus Christ came to earth. Before Moses Abel and Abraham equally recognized the need of a temporary animal sacrifice in place of the immediate death of the sinner. John the Baptist proclaimed Jesus as the Lamb of God, Who takes away the sin of the world! (John 1:29) Paul tells us that Christ our Passover is sacrificed for us. 1 Corinthians 5:7. Psalm 22, Isaiah 53 and the Book of Hebrews goes into great detail on this subject. Study these passages for more instruction, but for present purposes the point is that we belong to God not only by Creation but also by purchase through the shed blood of Jesus Christ and His death in our place for our sinfulness including particular sins. He owns us "lock, stock and barrel." *We are His people and the sheep of His pasture.* Psalm 100:3.

Before God humanity, including us, is unspeakably guilty. Romans 3:23 says in summary that *All have sinned and come short of the glory of God.* Romans 3:9-18 is a more detailed indictment of humanity collectively and individually.

To underscore how offensive we are to God in our natural state and to begin to understand how much our Lord Jesus paid to redeem us, we should consider John 3:14, where Jesus said, *And as Moses lifted up the serpent in the wilderness, even so must the Son of man be lifted up.* Our Lord Jesus was referring to Numbers 21, when God sent poisonous snakes among the people of Israel as both a punishment for their sin and as a graphic representation of their moral nature. (Indeed, one of the indictments of humanity in Romans 3:13 is that *the poison of asps* [the kind of snake that Cleopatra used to kill herself] *is under their lips.*) In Numbers 21 deliverance from the snakes was made available by looking at a portrayal of a snake raised up on a pole. Centuries later this became a picture of the crucifixion of Jesus Christ, Who, although perfect Himself, **took the place of a snake** in order to pay for the sins of many, including me. By birth nature I too was a snake and have remnants of that nature within me. Even today, we are familiar with the Texas expression "lower than a snake's belly." That's a measure of how low Jesus had to go to pay for my sin and save me.

The History Channel has done a series of documentaries on how crucifixion would have affected the physical body of Jesus Christ. It is horrific. The

Scriptures record His thirst, like the rich man in Luke 16:19-31 who felt his tongue on fire. We know that His skin was slashed severely by the scourging before the Cross, leading to blood loss and shock. His heartbeat was racing. When He was spiked to the Cross, several nerves would have been severed and would have pained him like perpetual "funnybones." He would have had to press upward on his spiked feet to breathe at all. Jesus endured the darkness for 3 hours, perhaps like that painful darkness that God inflicted on Egypt at the word of Moses. All of these things are elements of everlasting punishment for the moral snake who refuses God's offer of change and mercy. And this is not all. Jesus absorbed the just fury of God upon Himself and paid the full and entire price for my sin and for every believer (past, present and future) during the last hours of His life. He absorbed the judgment that every human snake deserves, including me. But the story does not end here. Jesus Christ rose from the dead and lives forever to pray for us. God accepted the suffering of His Son as payment in full for the sin of every believer.

All of these verses support the idea that the believer has been purchased by Jesus Christ and are owned by Him. *You are bought with a price; do not be the servants of men.* 1 Corinthians 7:23. *For you are bought with a price. Therefore glorify God in your body and in your spirit, which are God's.* 1 Corinthians 6:20. *For He [God] hath made Him [Jesus Christ] to be sin for us, Who knew no sin; that we might be made the righteousness of God in Him.* 2 Corinthians 5:21. *Let not sin therefore reign in your mortal body, that ye should obey it in the lusts thereof. Neither yield ye your members as instruments of unrighteousness unto sin:*

but yield yourselves unto God, as those that are alive from the dead, and your members as instruments of righteousness unto God. Romans 6:12-13.

When we speak of Jesus as being our Lord, we mean that He is sovereign beyond any earthly dictator. Hebrews 2:10 refers to Jesus as being the Captain of the believers' salvation. This is not the mid-range officer's rank as in modern armies or navies, but carries the sense that Captain-General did when the Duke of Marlborough led all allied forces against Louis XIV in an exhausting war. Marlborough was the unquestioned commander and military genius of that time, probably on a par with Alexander the Great, Julius Caesar and Napoleon in military skill. The superiority and authority of command of the Lord Jesus goes far beyond any military leader, however great. We, like Adam, are from earth and our bodies are subject to death. But the Lord Jesus, the Second Adam, came sinless and perfect from heaven. *The first man is of the earth, earthy: the second man is the Lord from heaven.* 1 Corinthians 15:47 See also John 6:32-41. The Lord Jesus is fundamentally above us even though He came in a human body like ours. He has absolute authority over us as no sinful human being can ever have regardless of the power that person may seem to have for the moment.

On this basis we should be willing to inquire in the Holy Bible about God's instructions for family life with a real willingness to obey what we find. Several issues arise:

1) How did marriage originate?

2) Is marriage exclusively between people of the opposite sex?

3) Under what circumstances, if any, is divorce permitted?

4) Can a person who has been divorced or widowed remarry?

5) What does God say about polygamy?

6) What are some guidelines for choosing a marriage partner?

7) Beyond family life, what about eternal life and the Last Judgment?

We will also touch on various other subjects as they link to our central themes.

[For the most part I have assumed in this book that the reader already knows that salvation is God's free gift to believers by grace alone through faith alone. For a very brief introduction to this topic, see Appendix A. Three contemporary authors who write extensively on this are R.C. Sproul, John McArthur and John Piper.]

CHAPTER 1

Origin Of Marriage

The Holy Scriptures make it clear in Genesis 2, starting in verse 18, that God originated marriage before sin. In Genesis 1:31, God saw that everything that He had created was (literally) "good good." Then Eve was created from Adam's rib in the Garden and introduced to Adam. Our Lord Jesus affirmed this in His great explanation of His reasoning on divorce. *"From the beginning it was not so [that men divorced their wives]."* Matthew 19:8. It is noteworthy that neither Adam nor Eve were ashamed to be naked at this point before sin had spoiled their Paradise.

After the Fall Eve bore children to Adam in Adam's fallen, sinful, mortal image. Cain and Abel were the first two. Then Cain murdered Abel, and Seth was born in Abel's place. Many other children followed.

Because of sin, no system of bearing and raising children works perfectly. But with knowledge of modern genetics we can observe some consequences of God's original design. Children would be raised by two parents, one male and one female. Each parent would have a unique although imperfect understanding of that child because each parent would have contributed half of that child's genes.

Permit me an illustration with one of my grandchildren. From my youngest days I like to complete my portion of one kind of food before I touch another, and so I continue until the end of the meal eating one portion at a time. My grandson has never lived with me and has not learned that habit from me. But he does the same thing. Perhaps this reflects some innate desire for order and system. But my daughter knows of my characteristics and realizes that this habit of her son has genetic roots. Even though some people might consider this odd, my daughter does not make an issue of it because she knows that it goes against the genetic grain of her child. I am confident that other parents have similar knowledge of family histories of various inherited characteristics that would give them an advantage over strangers in raising their children.

Another genetic consequence of God's design in bringing a man and a woman together to create a new human life is that (with the exception of identical twins) no two children are exactly alike in their genes. Each has a unique contribution to make, along with unique faults and weaknesses as well. These characteristics do allow populations to adjust genetically over time to their environments to maximize survival. James Behe has written extensively on this subject for those who desire to delve in detail into the science, using resistance of malaria and cellular structure in his most famous works in his argument that life has been designed.

I saw a bumper sticker which says that "Children need gender diversity." God also provided for this in His design. Single parents know how difficult it can be to fulfill the responsibilities of both father and mother without help from the opposite sex. One historical example of this was Abraham Lincoln, whose mother died when he was very young. Lincoln's father believed it his responsibility to find a suitable step-mother to help raise Abraham Lincoln and acted on that conviction about 4 months after the death of Lincoln's mother. Sarah Bush Johnston (then Lincoln) was a great influence for good in Lincoln's life after she married Lincoln's father. Not all step-parent relationships work this well, but this is an illustration of the benefit of both male and female influence to give children the best start possible.

Tragically, because of sin and death it is not always possible for two biological parents to raise children as God originally designed. The best policy in such cases is to get as close to God's original design as we can including genetic ties when possible or at least having a loving adoptive father and mother. Yet in some cases not even that is available. Think of the situation where Clara Hale of Harlem, New York starting taking in unwanted drug-addicted babies from mothers who could not or would not take care of them. With God's love supplemented by her own maternal love for babies who were not her legal responsibility many probable troubles were overcome for these children. I know that in my own family one person who bounced from place to place from a variety of causes including divorce and war. For most of the time that person did not live with either parent by the choice of the parents. Considering that the person was born in the United States, almost anything that could go wrong did go wrong. Some kids complain about working through college -- this person had to work through high school. For this person's childhood, Murphy was an optimist! Yet the Holy Spirit entered that person as a child and made all the difference in the world. That person is emotionally healthy despite the negative human factors through a strong faith in Christ. So there is hope through Jesus Christ in the worst of circumstances. Taking this example, the Lord Jesus does understand our ordeals. He, too was *"despised and rejected by men."* Isaiah 53:3. More generally, *For in that He Himself has suffered being tempted, He is able to help those that are tempted.* Hebrews 2:18.

At this point we should examine briefly the issue of Creation opposed to Darwinian macro-evolution. James Behe is a contemporary expert on this issue. John Whitcomb and Henry Morris have also dealt with geological issues, but when they wrote *The Genesis Flood* cellular biology was largely unknown. Darwinian macro-evolution is the belief that humanity evolved from less complex and less intelligent ancestors. Moreover, all of this evolution occurred randomly without any supreme intelligence. The logical conclusion which most macro-evolutionists hold is that all life has a single one-celled ancestor. This is directly opposed to the teaching of the Bible that God created all life forms, including humanity.

Biblical Creation does not dispute that life makes adaptations to its environment. Finches may change beaks. Local or even global environments do favor or disfavor certain genetic characteristics within a gene pool. But finches remain finches; viruses remain viruses although they may mutate and expand the forms of life that they infect; bacteria remain bacteria even as drug-resistant forms become prominent. Humans remain human even though minor genetic alterations may increase resistance to malaria. This is micro-evolution. This can be a powerful force but this is consistent with Creation. Micro-evolution must be distinguished from macro-evolution, which is an attempt to overthrow God as Creator.

Without going into detail, I will pose a few questions that I do not believe a macro-evolutionist can answer:

A) We can agree that things that do not live cannot evolve. Then how did water come to exist? What about iron, selenium, copper, salt, potassium and other vital non-living substances? Some macro-evolutionists will concede that Darwinian macro-evolution presupposes the existence of an environment conducive to life forms that we observe on earth. Others will search for an origin of the material universe that excludes God, again in the vain hope of finding an explanation of origins which makes humanity the supreme authority in the universe.

B) Neither oxygen nor carbon dioxide is capable of evolving. Assuming their presence, how can Darwinian evolution explain the existence of extensive and complex life forms that inhale oxygen and exhale carbon dioxide (mammals including human beings, for example) while other complex forms (plants of all descriptions) inhale carbon dioxide and exhale oxygen? This balance is essential to both -- the presence of either alone without the other would result in the suffocation of life. Are Darwinian macro-evolutionists really claiming simultaneous evolution of both types of life, however improbable that may be? If evolution is random, why do we observe that animals breathe in oxygen and and plants breath in carbon dioxide, instead of some plants and some animals using each method?

C) There are many instances of living things that depend on one another even though they are not closely related. Human beings benefit greatly from good bacteria in their intestines. This is one reason that yogurt is healthy. The Egyptian Plover cleans the teeth of crocodiles and gets its own food in the process. Bears eat fish, fruit and honey as a basic portion of their diet. Did fish, fruit bushes and flowers evolve simultaneously with bears, or before? Is it not true that predators are an instrument of any form of evolution? How did creatures evolve if there were no predators for them, for without predators how can natural selection operate? So did these and many other pairs of cooperative and antagonistic organisms evolve simultanously in a random manner?

D) Many plants as well as mammals reproduce sexually. In the case of animals, this means that a compatible male and female must have evolved simultaneously within traveling range of each other, but with matching but different reproductive parts. Sexually reproducing plants pose an even more difficult case because they cannot move. And how could male and female plants reproduce reliably without bees and other carriers of pollen? Yet how could bees have survived without flowers and fruit trees and bushes?

E) Why do living creatures stop reproducing and

then die? From an evolutionary perspective, it would be a great advantage to be able to reproduce perpetually and live perpetually. Yet death is universal. How does evolution explain this? In response to the evolutionary counter-question of why did God engineer imperfect organisms, you can answer that we do not now observe the original Creation but rather a fallen and inferior version marred by sin and consequential death. Romans 5:12;8:20-22

F) How did the force binding protons and neutrons into a nucleus, which is essential for atoms to exist, come into existence?

G) Why is the gravity on earth strong enough to hold a moon and an atmosphere suited to life but weak enough to permit humans to walk and to permit insects, butterflies and birds to fly?

H) Why is the percentage of oxygen sufficient to support life and exertion but not enough to make the entire earth a raging inferno when fire is set? (American space travel was originally conducted with pure oxygen but this was changed after a deadly fire in the space capsule killed 3 astronauts in 1967. Pure oxygen would turn a spark into an explosion and flash fire.)

I) This next observation deals with Noah's Flood rather than Creation. Some scientists are skeptical of the Flood based on the present height of the Himalayas. One point on which the Scriptures and Darwin macro-evolutionists do agree is that the earth's land mass was at one time a single continent. See Genesis 10:25 for a reference to the division of the continents *after* the Flood. There is no reason to suppose that the mountains were the same height at the time of the Flood as they are today.

This would reduce the amount of water required to flood the land mass, which then was unitary.

Macro-evolution can have deadly philosophical and political consequences, although most macro-evolutionists do not intend these consequences. Hitler argued from macro-evolutionary premises that it was right to kill off "weak" members of the human race for the benefit of the "strong." To Hitler, the "weak" included the insane, the disabled, Romany people, Slavs and Jews at the very bottom. To Hitler healthy Germans were the strongest and therefore the most fit to rule. When the Allies were overwhelming Hitler's Germany in 1945, he reasoned that the Germans were the weaker race and deserved to be destroyed completely. Even his Minister of Armaments, Albert Speer, frustrated Hitler's orders to destroy all German industry and infrastructure to speed the destruction of the "inferior" German people. Hitler remained logically consistent in his rigorous application of macro-evolutionary assumptions about the human race right up to his suicide. Contrast this with the Christian belief that all human beings are created by God and therefore protected by His Laws, such as the Ten Commandments.

Anyone reading Genesis 2 in a straightforward way would conclude that the original Biblical design for marriage and children had these features:

1) Marriage was between one man and one woman;

2) Sexual relations come after marriage and exclusively between the marriage partners. If this idea troubles you, read carefully Proverbs 2:16-22, all of Proverbs 5, Proverbs 6:23-35, all of Proverbs 7 and Proverbs 9:13-18. If God's warnings do not "take" on the first reading, continue to

study these passages because the issue they address affects a person all the way to the depths of the soul. For those who are breaking free from such sin, do not despair -- we will address 1 Corinthians 6:9-11 in detail;

3) Children were to be conceived, born and raised within marriage (since sin and death had not yet entered the universe, there were no exceptions in the original design);

4) Each parent would contribute 50% of the child's genetic heritage;

5) God is the Creator and giver of children. It is He Who somehow implants the soul and spirit into the conceived child. (Genesis 2:7; Job 12:10) Mankind did not try to determine the genetic make-up of the child. For reasons other than disease repair or medical treatment, attempts by humanity to control genetic design of children are an invasion of God's role in giving new life. God has given medicine to humanity, but there is a great moral difference between repairing a genetic defect which causes disease or even death and attempting to control the appearance or aptitudes of a child as one would select the various features of a new car. *It is He that has made us, and not we ourselves.* Psalm 100:3. By the same token God Himself created marriage.

CHAPTER 2

Biblical Teaching
Of Marriage: Polygamy

Polygamy seems such a strange subject to discuss. It is a man having more than one wife at the same time. To many Americans, it seems so remote in time that it is a non-issue. However, in the 21st century there may be a potential resurgence in the practice. Part of this is the rise of influence on the part of the Saudi royal family. Many of its male members practice polygamy today. Islamic scholars in the Middle East do at least permit the practice up to a maximum of 4 wives in certain circumstances.

Another issue concerning polygamy has its roots in American history. The Mormons as led by Joseph Smith and then Brigham Young taught and practiced polygamy. During the Civil War, the polygamy in the Utah Territory was ignored by Abraham Lincoln because of the crisis of southern secession and war. In the post-war period the issue was left on the back burner. When Utah had grown enough to be considered for statehood near 1890, Congress refused to admit the territory as a state so long as polygamy was permitted. Mormon elders of that time believed that they had received a fresh revelation from God to prohibit the practice, which had the effect of opening the way for Utah to be admitted to the Union as a full-fledged state. The prohibition was carried into effect. Some dissident Mormons left for Mexico or southeastern British Columbia in Canada rather than abandon polygamy. A few dissidents continued polygamous practices in remote areas within the United States where government presence was scarce. In modern America, Tom Green and Warren Jeffs are two men that have been punished by law because of their polygamy. A large majority of Mormons obeyed the decision of their elders and have renounced the polygamy of their founders. Like other states, Utah prohibits bigamy and polygamy.

As with all moral issues, we must find our truth in the Holy Scriptures. One item that must be acknowledged at the outset is that there is no Old Testament passage that forbids polygamy in direct, express terms. The first written instance of polygamy in Genesis is Lamech, who was also a vengeful man. It must be acknowledged that Abraham had intimate relations with Hagar with Sarah's initial consent and that Jacob was fooled into polygamy by his uncle Laban. There is no question that David and Solomon lived in polygamy. Therefore it is logically fair that we face and meet an argument phrased like this: if four great men such as Abraham, Jacob, David and Solomon were polygamous husbands, what's the problem with it?

Briefly one could also note Elkanah, husband of Hannah and father of Samuel. Hannah had great grief because she had no children but Elkanah's other wife did. Finally God did give Hannah a son, Samuel. Hannah's faith in a difficult situation was rewarded, but there is no credit reflected on Elkanah. The main story is found in 1 Samuel 1-2. One should note that Samuel was actually raised by Eli the High Priest and not by his natural father.

A closer examination of the Scriptures involved show us many of the problems. Abraham would up having to banish not only Hagar but also Ishmael, his oldest son. Genesis 21:10-14. All this occurred because of the jealousy involved with most polygamous relationships. In Abraham's case, the two wives could not even live together in the same house. Abraham also sent away the younger children he had after Sarah had died and Hagar was gone to Arabia with Ishmael. Genesis 25:1-6. Isaac, the son of God's promise, remained.

Jacob was caught in a cross-fire between Leah and Rachel. (The whole story is found in Genesis 29-35.) Rachel was best loved by Jacob, but Leah was more fertile. Genesis 30:1. Both wives used handmaids to try to increase the number of children of Jacob loyal to them. Leah even used mandrakes to make a deal with Rachel for Jacob's presence one night. Of Jacob's children, only Joseph was truly upright in own life. When you study the last speech of Jacob's life, note the many misdeeds and faults which he records of his own children. The first three children (Reuben, Simeon and Levi) were all set aside in favor of Judah as the ancestor of the Messiah ("when Shiloh comes" -- Genesis 49:10). When one examines the geneologies of the Lord Jesus and compares them with the account of Judah in Genesis 38, one sees that Judah was not upright either and had to be fooled by Tamar into raising up children to replace his sons who had died for their wickedness. As a whole, Jacob's family is not a model for family life.

David's family life was also a disaster. (Consider 2 Samuel 5-18 especially 12-13, for the main story.) He had multiple children by different wives. Amnon committed rape and incest with his sister Tamar. Absolom took the law into his own hands and killed Amnon and eventually rebelled against David. Adonijah refused to accept Solomon as David's successor and then asked for David's last companion as his wife. For this last rebellious request Adonijah was executed. Solomon multiplied David's bad example in taking 700 wives and 300 concubines. (See 1 Kings 11.) Solomon's wives induced him to participate in pagan worship. Solomon's son, King Rehoboam, thought that Solomon's heavy taxes were light and provoked perhaps the first recorded tax revolt, dividing Israel. (1 Kings 12.) No sensible person would want to imitate any of these families nor their results in the following generation.

The example of Ahab centuries later was even worse. (See 2 Kings 9-10.) He was married to Jezebel, but the seventy children that Ahab fathered could not all have come from Jezebel. These children came to a bad end through Jehu at God's express command. Jehu was a real-life Terminator. The fact that God commanded that Ahab's family be wiped out is a signal to the wickedness both of Ahab and of his offspring. Ahab's sister Athaliah massacred all the royal children of Judah, except that she missed one that was hidden for years in the Temple. (2 Kings 11.) This was truly an unsuccessful attempt by Satan through Athaliah to prevent the birth of Jesus Christ by killing all possible ancestors. If the rest of Ahab's family were like Athaliah, no wonder that God ordered the execution of his sons! In any case God permitted no remnant of Ahab to remain in order to stabilize the Northern Kingdom under Jehu's rule.

The prophet Malachi supported lifetime marriage to one woman in Malachi 2:14-15. While there are no words expressly mentioning polygamy, it is important that Malachi mentions <u>in the singular</u> "the wife of your youth." One of the main reasons was to bring up "a godly seed" -- godly children. I am not aware of Biblical references to polygamy after Ahab -- Malachi comes about 350-400 years later.

Moses did address polygamy in Exodus 21:7-10. Moses did not expressly forbid polygamy, although one could readily argue that the condition under which a man could take another wife in verse 10 amounts to an indirect prohibition because conditions are impossible to fulfill. A husband would have to maintain in full both his economic provisions for the first wife and his marital intimacy with her -- all while taking care of the second wife as well. Virtually no husband could do this! If one reads the books written by those who have lived under polygamy, the typical polygamous husband has no intention of treating all of his wives equally but instead of gratifying his own desires with whomever he will. In fact, the justifications for the practice that I have read claim that it is right for the strong man to sire as many children as he can. Family life assumes a structure like cattle in which one bull or stallion impregnates a number of mares or cows, and in the meantime maturing younger men lack legitimate marriage partners. We are not brute animals! This is not God's plan!

In the New Testament the Lord Jesus points us back in Matthew 19:1-10 to the origin of marriage -- the Creation itself. Obviously one man and one woman were originally created. However, he addressed divorce rather than polygamy because that was the question presented. The Apostle Paul does prohibit polygamy in 1 Corinthians 7:2: *Nevertheless, to avoid sexual immorality, let every man have his own wife, and let every woman have her own husband.* The singulars are critical here. Paul extends Jesus' general proposition that marriage must again be based on its foundation in Creation. He states that (with the exception of those who can live in singleness as explained later in 1 Corinthians 7) each man should have his own (singular) wife and that each woman should have her own (singular) husband. This was the condition in which God created Adam and Eve before sin entered the universe. When combined with 1 Corinthians 6:9-16, it is abundantly clear that men and women are to have one exclusive sexual partner unless celibate. Polygamy is indeed forbidden, and for our own good and the good of our children.

CHAPTER 3

Considerations On Selecting A Mate

What qualities would make a good spouse (if you are not already married)? The most basic answer for a person who has been reborn as a Christian is that a spouse <u>must</u> also be a believing Christian. The warning of 2 Corinthians 6:14 is vital:

> *Do not be unequally yoked together with unbelievers: for what fellowship does righteousness have with unrighteousness? And what communion does light have with darkness?*

This principle has broader application than just marriage, such as business partnerships also, but it applies to marriage most of all. A marriage between a believer and a non-believer is fraught with trouble because the partners are constantly pulling at cross purposes. Such marriages may arise when one member of a pre-existing marriage becomes a Christian, but a Christian should never knowingly and voluntarily enter such a relationship. 1 Corinthians 7 and 1 Peter 3:1-2 give instructions on how to handle this difficult situation when it arises.

But not every Christian man would make a good marriage partner for every Christian woman, nor vice versa. One basic trait for every prospective Christian spouse is that they themselves and any prospective mate already love the Bible and read it regularly. This is not so simple as it sounds; the ignorance of the Scriptures in many churches ranges from troubling to tragic. Another fundamental trait is that every Christian, specifically including those seeking marriage, must develop a life of prayer. Do not count on a mate developing a good habit from nowhere after marriage, because this rarely happens. People seeking marriage naturally put their best foot forward. One should count on discovering faults that were not apparent during courtship; it is rare to find virtues that did not appear during courtship. But while what I am saying is realistic most of the time, do not lose faith or hope. *With men it is impossible, but with God all things are possible.* Matthew 19:26.

I know that there are rare cases where God unites a man and a woman almost as one heart and one mind extremely rapidly. This has happened to me. I had prayed that God would choose a mate for me as He had directed Abraham's servant to choose a wife for Isaac in Genesis 24. The Lord most mercifully answered in less than a week. However, one should also note that my wife and I were both over 40 at the time and both of us had long backgrounds in the Scriptures. After but a few minutes I knew that the lady across the table knew our Lord Jesus and loved God's Word, which were the most critical points. Even so, we waited about 6 weeks until the marriage had been performed before we spent even one night together. We had to deal rapidly with financial issues in finding a home where we could live after our marriage, so we could look at how each of us handled a major financial decision. With younger people who have less experience, I think that such rapid action is even rarer than among the more mature. For the majority, there is a process that involves both emotion and thought.

From the standpoint of human responsibility, there are certain unities that are important for the foundation of a solid marriage. This is one aspect of life where it is important to use our minds as well as listen to our hearts. We have all examined one essential unity: a <u>common conversion.</u> There is no spiritual union or fellowship between a person who is alive to God and another person who is spiritually dead, a spiritual corpse. (If necessary, review Ephesians 2.) For emphasis I repeat, if you are a Christian and are not yet married, do not marry an unbeliever. However, I should also point out that God has given marriage to all of humanity, including those who are ignorant of Him. Marriages occurred right up to the rains that floated Noah's Ark. Marriages among unbelievers are essential to the well-being of society even though they lack spiritual content in the Biblical and Christian sense of that word.

For any couple considering marriage, a <u>common communion</u> is essential. Each partner must be comfortable in sharing spiritual truth and even spiritual struggles with the other. One needs more than an agreement on Biblical content -- one needs a natural joint worship of the Savior together. Each partner must be able to trust the other with intimate truth spiritually before the wedding and before opening themselves bodily to the other.

Another essential part of the foundation of a Christian marriage is a <u>common calling.</u> At the very least, the man and woman need to sense compatible and complementary callings so that their lives can mesh together as one team. If one person of a prospective couple has a call to South America and another a call to Africa or to the United States, there is a basic problem that needs to be resolved before the wedding rather than later. I have heard of one person who married a man training to be a pastor even though she emphatically did not want to be a minister's wife. When the man continued on his path, shipwreck in the marriage followed. It is unlikely that the calling of a man and of his wife would be identical, but they must complement one another or else there is some misunderstanding of God's will that needs to be prayed through.

Another aspect of a common calling that needs to be examined is the time that work will compel a prospective couple to spend apart compared to the time that they will be able to spend together. People differ in their ability to withstand temporary separations due to work. For example, a long-haul trucker or a traveling salesperson may be "on the road" for several days at a time. High-paid professionals frequently are required to stay late at the office. Are the parties' work plans and genuine needs compatible? If not, some change needs to be made. This issue becomes more acute if children are born because both parents need to share their upbringing.

There also needs to be a <u>common commitment.</u> Christian marriage is designed to last a lifetime. There should be no reservations about each party's intent to "forsake all others" -- not only former love interests but even parents and family -- and to give oneself unreservedly to the other. There is no room for any romance in marriage except with one's mate. When the marriage hits rough water, as it will for discipleship purposes even when the couple is following God's will, neither divorce nor permanent or even trial separation should ever be on the table. Even in an argument, threats of this kind should be totally out of bounds and never made unless adultery has occurred in fact. *"Whom God has joined together, let no man put asunder."* Matthew 19:6. (I believe that 1 Corinthians 7 does also permit divorce when one mate refuses to live without violence with the other in the same house, but such circumstances should never arise between believers.)

Both men and women contemplating marriage should study Ephesians 5:22-33, 1 Timothy 3:1-12, Titus 1:5-14 and Proverbs 31 to examine both themselves and their intended mate. The Scriptures do teach that if there is no other way to resolve a disagreement, that the woman should follow her husband unless he is ordering her to sin. For example, see 1 Peter 3:6. Then the woman needs to ask herself honestly whether she has enough confidence in God's choice of this man to follow him when his plans are contrary to her judgment. Conversely, the man needs to ask himself honestly whether he trusts his prospective wife's wisdom to complement his own.

Also, he needs to ask himself whether he can trust her to administer the household in his absence. Is he willing if necessary to sacrifice his own desires to care for her genuine spiritual needs? 1 Peter 3:7. Since the man under Christ is supposed to be the spiritual leader in the home, is he capable in terms of Biblical knowledge of teaching spiritual truth to each member of the family? Has each member of the relationship considered the other as a parent? We are commanded in James to be "*swift to hear, slow to speak and slow to anger.*" James 1:19. Likewise, an elder in Titus 1:7 must not be quick to get angry. Conversely, does a prospective wife have wisdom and the law of kindness in her speech? (Proverbs 31:26) An uncontrolled temper is a disaster anywhere but especially in a marriage. Consider these verses on this subject:

> *It is better to dwell in the wilderness, than with a contentious and an angry woman. Proverbs 21:19*

> *Make no friendship with an angry man; and with a furious man you shalt not go; Lest you learn his ways, and get a snare to your soul. Proverbs 22:24-25*

> *An angry man stirs up strife, and a furious man abounds in transgression. Proverbs 29:22*

Another important question is whether one's intended mate is proud or willing to listen and learn. There are many verses on this subject, but this one applies well to both male and female: *A man's pride shall bring him low:*

but honour shall uphold the humble in spirit. Proverbs 29:23.

How cheerful are you? How sober-minded are you? The Scriptures commend both, but maintaining both is not easy -- without the Holy Spirit it is impossible. *The joy of the Lord is your strength.* Nehemiah 8:10. Yet we are also commanded to be sober not only in the sense of avoiding intoxication by any mind-altering substance but also in the sense of being honest, objective and level-headed in judgment. Romans 12:3. It is impossible to be sober-minded when you are not sober in the physical sense, so naturally you should look for the nearest exit if your intended partner even occasionally becomes intoxicated or uses tobacco, much less marijuana or worse, in my view. It is perfectly possible to avoid intoxicants and yet succumb to egotism, which in the context of Romans 12 is the opposite of being sober-minded and can be just as destructive as drugs. Often being sober-minded means acknowledging how short we fall from God's standard of holiness. *Blessed are they that mourn, for they shall be comforted.* Matthew 5:4. Nehemiah's audience was mourning; it needed to be encouraged. No Christian should be an ultimate pessimist because Jesus Christ and His righteousness will triumph when all is said and done. But we need to be sober-minded about ourselves and also about our intended marriage partner. Yet we should be cheerful because of God's triumphant grace and love. This is another dimension which I would consider when marriage is in view.

Many verses that we usually consider in relationships within the church can be applied with profit between husband and wife or between prospective marriage partners as well. *"Let nothing be done through strife or vainglory; but in lowliness of mind let each esteem others better than themselves. Look not every man on his own things, but everyone also on the things of others."* Philippians 2:3-4. *"We then that are strong ought to bear the infirmities of the weak, and not to please ourselves. Let every one of us please his neighbor for his good to edification."* Romans 15:1-2. I cannot imagine a closer "neighbor" than a spouse. Bearing in mind that marriage partners become "one flesh" (Matthew 19:5; 1 Corinthians 6:16 -- this is even closer than the "one body" relationship of the church of Ephesians 4:16) meditate on what Paul wrote through the Spirit in Ephesians 4:1-6 with your prospective or actual mate in mind:

> *I therefore, the prisoner of the Lord, beseech you that you walk worthy of the calling wherewith ye are called,with all lowliness and meekness, with longsuffering, forbearing one another in love; endeavouring to keep the unity of the Spirit in the bond of peace. There is one body, and one Spirit, even as ye are called in one hope of your calling; one Lord, one faith, one baptism; one God and Father of all, who is above all, and through all, and in you all.*

Virtually all of Ephesians 4 & 5 can be applied specially to the husband-wife relationship which is described more fully in Ephesians 5:22-33, although those principles apply to unmarried people as well. Consider as a thumbnail sketch Ephesians 4:25-27: *"Wherefore putting away lying, speak every man truth with his neighbor: for we are members one of another. Be you angry, and sin not: let not the sun go down upon your wrath; neither give place to the devil."* After condemning theft, Paul continues:

> *"Let no corrupt communication proceed out of your mouth, but that which is good to the use of edifying, that it may minister grace unto the hearers. And grieve not the Holy Spirit of God, whereby ye are sealed unto the day of redemption. Let all bitterness, and wrath, and anger, and clamour, and evil speaking, be put away from you, with all malice. And be kind one to another, tenderhearted, forgiving one another, even as God for Christ's sake has forgiven you."*
> *Ephesians 4:29-32*

Examine yourself spiritually as if you were examining your body for some abnormality that might indicate physical disease. If you are considering marriage, then honestly consider your intended mate also. If you need to rebuke an intended or actual mate, please do it gently. Pray over these things. No mate will ever be perfect, but are the foundations of these qualities and conduct visible now? You can also use the same basic thought process to other passages of Scripture that give standards for conduct within the church.

Another broad area to consider before marriage is the the handling of money. One can start with the 10th Commandment: *You shall not covet.* If you avoid desiring things that you cannot afford and are not ashamed to lag behind your contemporaries in accumulating "stuff", you can avoid many financial strains. If one really needs something, buy it used or at a discount if at all. I agree with Dave Ramsay's basic advice against buying new cars (except in rare cases where normal price patterns are distorted or necessary mileage is truly tremendous, as with a salesman who travels long distances by car as part of his work). Consider this verse, especially when applied to a man, *"He that is lazy in his work is brother to him who is a great waster."* Proverbs 18:9. It is also desirable to keep debt to a minimum and to avoid it when reasonably possible. *"The rich rules over the poor, and the borrower is servant to the lender."* Proverbs 22:7. While there are exceptions, in most marriages in my legal experience (which includes major experience in both domestic relations and bankruptcy) men earn in the range of 60%-75% of the total family income when both parties work. While again there is variation, more women administer the family treasury than men. Again referring to my legal experience, if either prospective marriage partner has trouble reading financial documents or understanding financial concepts, the partner who has this trouble is far more likely to be the man in 21st century America. I have represented many a man who is skilled with his hands but has no clue with a checkbook, loan documents or a financial program. If you are such a person, it is especially important that you prize honesty and trustworthiness in your prospective mate. The gaps in your knowledge expose you to being "cheated" by a free-spending spouse (especially if drugs are a hidden problem) and then being stuck with the essential bills that have fallen behind. Some women are also in this situation, but that is less frequent in my experience. If the marriage is going to follow the most usual pattern, it is highly important to have a hard-working man and a frugal wife to keep an even financial keel. At the very least, both spouses have to restrain their spending and neither can be lazy. (Note: keeping a home and raising children can be a full-time job in itself and is not to be despised or valued lightly if done conscientiously.)

One signal about financial responsibility is tithing and a prospective mate's attitude toward tithing. Going back as far as Abram (to become Abraham) in Genesis 14, he tithed to Melchizedek, whom I believe to have been a pre-birth appearance of the Son of God (although scholars debate this). Tithing therefore pre-dates the giving of the Law. Our Lord Jesus commended the Pharisees for their tithing even when He was condemning their gross omissions of justice, mercy and faith. Matthew 23:23; Luke 11:42. While some scholars debate this, I can find nothing in the command to bring one's offerings on the first day of the week *as God has prospered* (1 Corinthians 16:2) as repealing the tithe. For a further Scripture, read Malachi 3:8-12 for God's condemnation of those who did not tithe under the Law and for His promise of blessing for those who do. While the blessing to one who tithes cheerfully (2 Corinthians 9:7) is not always monetary, it is always worthwhile. While one may start tithing by command, one should seek in his or her heart to progress to willing giving and then to cheerful giving. This is one area where I need to grow, especially in the comparatively hard times we face as I write. In choosing a mate, attitude toward tithing is usually a window in many aspects of your prospective mate's character.

I have not mentioned virginity to this point, even

though people entering their first marriage will all be virgins if they have been obedient to the Scriptures. This is vitally important, but God can overcome past failures in this as in other respects. Marrying someone who has been sexually uncontrolled in the past and has no sorrow about it is an almost surefire recipe for a broken heart and perhaps a fatal disease. But Rahab of Jericho became a wife in the lineage of Jesus Christ. Martin Luther insisted on marriage for monks and nuns who were leaving their cloisters because he knew full well that they had not been able to handle celibacy and in fact had indulged forbidden lusts as monks and nuns. To forbid marriage to people with this background would have made a bad problem worse. 1 Timothy 4:3. Faithful, monogamous marriage was and is the God-given remedy for the inability of most mature adults short of very advanced age to live celibate.

I also take what I believe to be a Biblical position that is highly controversial in cases where there is existing cohabitation and then someone asks a Christian what to do about it. If neither party is legally married to someone else, then I believe that they should marry each other, even though there may be many difficulties to be faced. They have already become "one flesh" according to the teachings of 1 Corinthians 6. Furthermore, the Old Testament in Exodus 22:16-17 calls for marriage in such cases. I think this situation is similar to that mentioned in the previous paragraph and should be handled under the same principles. Sometimes a new believer or even a relapsed believer will, like a golfer, have to play their life where they have struck the ball in a very unfavorable position. Let such a person start obeying the Scriptures now through the grace of God and trust that He will work right out of wrong as He has done so often.

My checklist is only a start; it is not close to exhaustive. Romance is great, but it is not enough by itself to sustain a marriage. This is especially true when difficulties arise, as they will. I do not mean to exclude mutual attraction as one indicator for marriage, but I am counseling that you use your mind as well as your heart in considering a marriage partner. No prospective marriage partner will be perfect, but these and similar questions should be asked beforehand and both prospective partners should be reasonably sure that the faults of the other party are bearable.

I have not concentrated on the most usual questions that people ask about a prospective spouse, such as (1) Is he or she rich? (2) Is he or she handsome or pretty? (3) What does he or she do for a living? It is essential, especially for a man, to have a skill at which one can earn a living except in unusual cases such as retirees or the independently wealthy. But many people have these and still make terrible mates. Look at all the examples of failed marriages among political leaders, sports figures and the entertainment industry. Lots of money is no guarantee of a happy marriage. Spiritual factors are the most critical.

Permit me one example from history. A brilliant aristocratic English couple couldn't be bothered with the day-to-day responsibilities of raising their children, so they hired a nanny. He became Chancellor of the Exchequer, the equivalent of our Secretary of the Treasury and the #2 person in the government. She was a beautiful horsewoman and wealthy socialite. The nanny providentially was a devout Christian and taught the faith to the two boys. She simply raised two brothers as a mother would. History records that this humble nanny died without enough money to pay for a funeral. One of her "sons" paid the cost. Yet she did more for England than almost anyone in her generation. Why? One of the brothers was named Jack. The other brother is now known as Sir Winston Churchill, who was used by God to deliver England from Hitler and the Nazis.

CHAPTER 4

Bible Teaching: Parenting

The Holy Scriptures have much to say about raising children. For detailed teaching from a person who both believes the Scriptures and has expert specialized training, I would recommend the work of Dr. James Dobson, starting with <u>Dare to Discipline</u>. No book other than the Bible is perfect, but Dr. Dobson will be miles better than the popular culture or current "feel-good" books that take no consideration of the sin nature embedded with all human beings (except Jesus Christ Himself), including children. Not even babies are free of sin. *Foolishness is bound in the heart of a child, but the rod of correction shall drive it far from him.* Proverbs 22:15.

Principle 1: Do not be afraid to administer controlled physical discipline on children.

Notice that Solomon, the wisest of sinful human beings, under the control of the Holy Spirit mentions the "rod of correction." This obviously refers to an object hard enough to administer stinging pain. Solomon is not endorsing inflicting serious injury on a child. There are people who vent uncontrolled anger on a child and do serious damage. When such facts are proved, such parents or other people should be punished severely by the law. On the other hand, spanking on the buttocks for a short time rarely if ever causes such injury (except for a child with hemophilia or a similar disease). The mere presence of a bruise on the buttocks by itself should not be considered a badge of child abuse. Depending on the nature and gravity of a child's offense, it may be a duty of a parent to administer enough force to leave a bruise on the buttocks in order to help train the soul and mind. *The blueness of a wound cleanses away evil: so do stripes the inward parts of the belly.* Proverbs 20:30. I have heard one trial judge who later became a justice of the Virginia Supreme Court state from the bench that his father disciplined him with a riding crop and that it did him no harm at all. He indicated that later he understood that his father was acting properly as a parent. Matters that are especially serious for a child's character development, such as lying, cheating and stealing, should be met with serious pain (although not serious injury) as soon as discovered.

Another illustration: I know of a child who in his second year of high school was caught cheating on a quiz. He told his father after work that same day. The father still took a belt to the buttocks, although the father cut the strokes in half because the son volunteered the truth. So far as is known to human knowledge, that student did not cheat again. Nearly two years later, another boy in the same at the same school was caught cheating on a final exam. That cheating cost him and his parents a scholarship worth close to $10,000 in today's dollars which went instead to the boy who had been spanked earlier in high school. To expand the lesson further, cheating as an adult can cost a job (for example, being fired for inflating a resume) or even one's freedom (for example, cheating on taxes or financial statements). Do not be afraid to punish dishonesty (lying, cheating, stealing, etc.) severely enough to leave a lasting impression in the child's mind and soul that personal dishonesty is to be avoided at all costs. The only exceptions that the Scriptures allow are in warfare (for example, Rahab in Joshua 2) or in resisting a tyrant (for example, Exodus 1 & 2 when Pharaoh commanded mass murder or in hiding Jews from the Nazis).

In tragic situations where a particular child has been abused to the point where spanking creates terror in the child because of previous abuse, some other method of physical discomfort may have to be substituted for the usual application of the "board of education to the seat of understanding." But temporary pain administered in love without lasting harm is still an effective teacher.

Some professionals say that any corporal punishment is child abuse. I have heard this from the witness stand. The Scriptures teach that the absence of discipline, normally including corporal punishment on occasion, shows that the parent hates the child. Failing to correct a child when it is called for does harm the child, perhaps severely. *He that spares his rod hates his son: but he that loves him chastens him from time to time.* Proverbs 13:24. *Chasten your son while there is hope, and let not your soul spare for his crying.* Proverbs 19:18. *Do not withhold correction from the child: for if you beat him with the rod, he shall not die. You shall beat him with the rod, and shalt deliver his soul from hell.* Proverbs 23:13-14.

Principle 2: Discipline should be in proportion to the offense.

Not all corrective discipline has to be physical, and not all spanking needs to be with an object. In many cases a corrective word is enough. *A wise son hears his father's instruction: but a scorner does not hear rebuke.* Proverbs 13:1. *The ear that hears the reproof of life abides among the wise.* Proverbs 15:31. *As an earring of gold, and an ornament of fine gold, so is a wise reprover upon an obedient ear.* Proverbs 25:12. In some other cases a quick slap on the back of the hand (for example, the toddler sampling electrical outlets) may be sufficient. For minor disobedience spanking with the hand may be sufficient. My own practice was to reserve an object for the most grave cases, of which I thank God there were few. As Art Linkletter (who loved the Lord Jesus and had a special love and rapport with children and also lived an especially long life -- his books on children would be worth reading if you can find them) pointed out, no two children are the same, and my own suggestions may not work in someone else's family. Only the Scriptures themselves are infallible. The entire structure of the Law of Moses has punishments proportioned to the gravity of the disobedience, and in miniature this should be reflected in how parents deal with children.

Principle 3: You must be in control of yourself before you discipline your child.

I have observed situations where a parent was so frustrated with a child that substantive communication between them was blocked. The parent was yelling at the child, but the child simply was not hearing what was being said. The child understood that the parent was angry and frustrated, but the lack of self-control on the part of the parent prevented the child from understand why. All the child could "hear" was the parent's emotion. At the same time the parent could not "hear" what the child was trying to say in response. The parent's emotions blocked any comprehension of the child's response and whether that response had any justification or not. A calm tone of voice is most effective in correction because it focuses more on the content than the feelings of the parent.

I heard a missionary story about a toddler. His father was some distance away and called to him to get flat on the ground. Then he said to crawl toward him, and then to get up and run toward him. The son obeyed. At first these instructions seemed nonsensical, but then the visitor observed a snake hanging out of a tree and preparing to strike at the son. Neither the father nor the son panicked. Through the mercy of God and then obedience the son escaped the snake in the physical sense. I hope and pray that the same would prove true for you in the spiritual sense also.

I would not base this point on fallible human observation, including my own. The Scriptures stress the importance of self-control; I am simply applying this principle to raising children. *He that is slow to anger is better than the mighty; and he that rules his spirit than he that takes a city.* Proverbs 16:32. More modern versions (for example, the Schofield KJV) translate the King James word "temperance" as "self-control" because after the King James version was translated the word "temperance" has taken a meaning connected with abstaining from alcohol and other intoxicants. With that understanding of language change between the King James translation and today's English, consider the following passages referring to self-control as they apply to raising and training your children for Jesus Christ:

> *But the fruit of the Spirit is love, joy, peace, longsuffering, gentleness, goodness, faith, meekness, temperance: against such there is no law. Galatians 5:22-23.*

> *And beside this, giving all diligence, add to your faith virtue; and to virtue knowledge; and to knowledge temperance; and to temperance patience; and to patience godliness; And to godliness brotherly kindness; and to brotherly kindness charity. 2 Peter 1:5-7*

> [The word virtue has a connotation of courage, and the word for charity now means love rather than charity in the modern restricted sense of assistance to the poor or sick.]

Dr. Dobson gave an illustration in one of his taped seminars on marriage and raising children of a teacher who violated the principle of self-control. When her class drove her to her wit's end, she would stand on a desk and blow a whistle. Her students soon learned how to drive her to that point. When they decided that they wanted some comic relief, they would "push the teacher's buttons" and get the desired spectacle. Who was in control here? The students were because of the teacher's lack of self-control. In truth they all paid a price for the teacher's lack of self-control. The students received an inferior example and learned how to manipulate others for wrongful purposes. The teacher had an awful time and learning was reduced. Parents without self-control can be caught in the same trap.

Principle 4: If you want to teach your children effectively, show them as well as tell them.

Our Lord Jesus was especially severe on those that He knew to be hypocrites. For an extended example, see Matthew 23. Our Lord indicted the Pharisees of His time in verse 3 (I have added the underline): *All therefore whatsoever they bid you observe, that observe and do; but do not you after their works: <u>for they say, and do not.</u>* For another passage with a similar idea, read Matthew 21:28-32. There follows a succession of woes pronounced, which sounds similar in structure to the woes of Revelation. Let us all pause to examine ourselves: do we say, and do not? If so, let us repent right now.

Children are swift to detect phonies. If a parent smokes tobacco or uses drugs and yet instructs his or her children not to do so, children are quick to challenge parents on the inconsistency between their words and their behavior. If the good advice is not backed by example, children are far more likely to follow the example than to follow the advice. So often, the children will go further in the wrong direction than the parents. David had several wives; Solomon had 700 wives and 300 concubines. Solomon taxed heavily near the breaking point; Rehoboam promised taxation that would be still heavier and chastening with scorpions instead of with whips. 1 Kings 12:14. Shakespeare wrote to the effect that the good that people do dies with them but that their evil lives on after them. Ultimately, through the power and grace of God, Shakespeare will be proved wrong as to believers in Jesus Christ. As Micah 7:19 says, *He will turn again, He will have compassion upon us; He will subdue our iniquities; and You will cast all their sins into the depths of the sea.* With believers' sins buried in the depths of the sea, their righteous deeds live on. As Revelation 14:13 says:

> *And I heard a voice from heaven saying unto me, Write, Blessed are the dead which die in the Lord from now on: Yes, saith the Spirit, that they may rest from their labors; and their works do follow them.*

But while the curse is reversed in the final triumph of the righteous Jesus Christ over all the works of Satan (1 John 3:8), in terms of earthly human responsibility of parents toward children Shakespeare is right much of the time. Children follow and often extend the evil example of their parents. This is sometimes true even in families of faith, as in the case of David and Solomon. There are times when children refuse to follow even a parent who shows a consistent pattern of right and holy living, as was the case with Samuel's children. 1 Samuel 8:3. But it is far better to show the consistent example of doing what's right to back up our advice than to struggle to undo evil patterns in our children to which we have contributed by our own example. We will fall short, so we must always pray for God's mercy and power to fix where we fail. But we must strive to live as close to God's Word as we can to give an essentially consistent example to our children.

Principle 5: Encourage Endurance In Your Children

Most athletes know of the need for physical endurance to enjoy sports. We also are aware of a growing problem of obesity among our children, which both causes and contributes to a lack of physical endurance among the current generation of children. Exercise, which builds endurance, is essential to the physical health of our children. So it is spiritually as well. As the Apostle Paul wrote through the Holy Spirit:

> *Don't you know that they which run in a race run all, but one receives the prize? So run, that you may obtain. And every man that strives for the mastery is temperate in all things. Now they do it to obtain a corruptible crown; but we an incorruptible. I therefore so run, not as uncertainly; so fight I, not as one that beats the air. But I keep under my body, and bring it into subjection: lest that by any means, when I have preached to others, I myself should be a castaway. 1 Corinthians 9:24-27.*

When I was a teen, I wrestled for 5 years and learned the value of endurance and perseverance. My best result was to finish second to my own teammate in a 6-team tournament at the end of my senior season. He went on to be a state champion. The beginnings of many victories on the wrestling mat were in the training room. So it is that reading and studying the Holy Scriptures is part of the necessary training for the temptations of life.

> *For we wrestle not against flesh and blood, but against principalities, against powers, against the rulers of the darkness of this world, against spiritual wickedness in high places. Ephesians 6:12*

Lessons from physical wrestling prepared me to accept the hardships of spiritual wrestling. Douglas MacArthur, the Army leader of the drive against Japan and later its military governor after World War 2 with distinction, likewise believed that for future officers of the Army that athletic competition laid foundations for military victories later.

This idea must be tempered with the knowledge that athletic ability varies widely among children and that some kids will never succeed in athletic competition, although I believe that all kids need some form of vigorous exercise unless special physical challenges make this impossible. I knew one such classmate who was the absolute worst athlete one can imagine except for those with special physical challenges. He was a weakling with very slow gross muscle reflexes and poor coordination. But he excelled academically, especially in mathematics and science, and went on as an adult to a career in oncology and in researching drugs that fight cancer. He was as good a musician as he was terrible as an athlete. I knew other students who loved drama and spent hours rehearsing and learning lines or even prompting. Not everyone will learn from athletics, but all must learn from sustained practice at something. It can be athletics, music, karate, dance or something else wholesome for which the child has some aptitude and enjoyment. Everyone must learn to excel at something, because that is how anyone will earn a living. You would not want to call the worst plumber or car mechanic in your town; rather you would call one of the best. The same is true of an interior decorator or real estate agent. Your child must learn along with endurance the principle of excellence, as it is written, *"And whatsoever you do in word or deed, do all in the name of the Lord Jesus, giving thanks to God and the Father by Him."* Colossians 3:17. *"Whether therefore ye eat, or drink, or whatsoever ye do, do all to the glory of God."* 1 Corinthians 10:31.

As a parent, you need to both teach and show the principle of excellence to all of our children, both male and female. Even if an adult is not going to work outside the home, that person will need to excel as a Christian and as a mate (if married) and in carrying out responsibilities at home. In striving to teach excellence, we need to remember that a child has a calling from God that may be different from our own and indeed quite different from our original concept of that child's life. What if our child is called to another continent by God? Or to medicine when we wanted that child to be an athlete, or vice versa? As a child gets closer to adulthood, this is one area where we may indeed have to "let go and let God" direct the older child as he or she matures to his or her own calling.

Some of our children may serve in the military. But spiritually, all of us believers are soldiers of Jesus Christ. *You therefore endure hardness as a good soldier of Jesus Christ.* 2 Timothy 2:3. As such, we must endure training and even chastening. *If you endure chastening, God deals with you as with sons; for what son is he whom the father chastens not?* Hebrews 12:7. Endurance is a necessary consequence of conversion, given training and time. *And you shall be hated of all men for my name's sake: but he that shall endure unto the end, the same shall be saved.* Mark 13:13. This also appears in Matthew 10:22 and Matthew 24:13. Compare this with Mark 4:17 where the "stony ground" hearer of the Parable of the Sower is offended at the first sign of persecution and bears no fruit. That person clearly ends up lost. The same parable is found in Matthew 13. The genuine Christian will endure in the end even though his or her strength has its breaking point. God knows this and will keep temptation below this level. 1 Corinthians 10:13 promises this:

> *There has no temptation taken you but such as is common to man: but God is faithful, who will not permit you to be tempted above that you are able; but will with the temptation also make a way to escape, that you may be able to bear it.*

Consider Jude 24 and Romans 8:28-39 for further assurance of God's preserving strength. Learning endurance as children will prepare us to be mature adult believers in Jesus Christ.

Endurance is also necessary for joy. *"Blessed is the man that endures temptation: for when he is tried, he shall receive the crown of life, which the Lord has promised to them that love him."* James 1:12. *Behold, we count them happy which endure. You have heard of the patience of Job, and have seen the end of the Lord; that the Lord is very pitiful, and of tender mercy.* James 5:11. Job's trial was unusually severe, involving the loss of 10 children and being sick to the edge of death with awful pain. Financially he lost a fortune. But God saw him through and Job ended up a thoroughly joyful man. Job's wife advised him to "*curse God and die*" (Job 2:9) but Job endured the struggle and received blessing from God both on earth and in heaven. His wife shared the blessing of Job's restoration.

Endurance is another quality that parents have to show their children as well as teach. I have only sketched an outline for a thorough study on endurance. The book of Job would be a start, as would a study of David's life and a study of Hebrews 11, the faith chapter. Moses also endured tremendous hardships. The Book of Acts and the Corinthian letters stress the trials and endurance of Paul. And the Lord Jesus Christ endured more than anyone, by far. *"For consider Him that endured such contradiction of sinners against Himself, lest ye be wearied and faint in your minds."* Hebrews 12:3. For those with a computer, do a word search in the Bible on "endure" and "endurance." Such studies will give you far more on the subject than I have sketched -- there is enough in the Scriptures for an entire book on that subject alone.

God spoke of Himself to Moses in Exodus 3:15 as *"the God of Abraham, the God of Isaac and the God of Jacob."* Abraham is celebrated as the intellectual and spiritual father of the people of faith. Romans 4 is an example. Isaac was a man of peace, a good neighbor who avoided quarrels when possible. He apparently was thoughtful (Genesis 24:63). By digging wells (no small job in those days without machinery, and what if Isaac and the workmen had stopped one foot too soon?) he enabled later generations to live in the land where there are dry seasons that last months, like California climates. But why the God of Jacob? After all, Jacob was at best a shrewd trader who persuaded Esau to sell his birthright for a single meal. He deceived his father Isaac into giving him the blessing that Isaac had intended for Esau. God allowed the deception to succeed because Isaac was planning to act contrary to His own word to his wife Rebecca (Genesis 25:23 -- Jacob was the younger, Esau the older). There are at least some attractive qualities to Abraham and Isaac, though of course both were sinners.

As a matter of history Jacob was renamed Israel (meaning prince with God) and was the father of the founders of the 12 tribes of Israel. But what good quality did Jacob show? If you read Jacob's story in Genesis, do you ever find him quitting? When he got a dose of his own deception in getting Leah instead of Rachel, did he quit? During 20 years of serving Laban outdoors with 10 wage changes, did Jacob quit? When his relationship with Laban frayed beyond repair, did Jacob quit? When Jacob was to meet Esau, did Jacob quit? Above all, when Jacob was wrestling with the angel (Genesis 32:24 and following -- I believe that Jacob was actually wrestling with the Son of God before He came to earth in human flesh), did Jacob quit even after his leg (perhaps his hip) was dislocated? No! With Jacob's past, God still chose to identify Himself by Jacob's name. It is Jacob's persistence and endurance that is to be celebrated. Jacob did not quit even when he thought that his favorite son Joseph was dead. Jacob did not quit through drought. On the last day of his life Jacob prophesied the future of the twelve tribes of Israel. If Abraham is an example of faith, and Isaac an example of peace, then Jacob is an example of endurance and perseverence. Every generation of Christians, and especially the terminal generation before the coming of the Lord Jesus Christ, will need endurance and perseverence to spiritually triumph over the enemy of souls. In this quality Jacob is a model short of the Lord Jesus Christ. In this quality we want our children to be like Jacob.

CHAPTER 5
Biblical Teaching: Abortion

Before we deal directly with the issue of abortion, we should as an introduction deal briefly with an issue of words which frequently conceals a spiritual trap. One frequently reads or hears of a Biblical "tradition." This is in itself at least a caution light, because the word "tradition" tends to bring the Bible down to the level of other sources of teaching. Commentaries on the Old Testament by various rabbis were in circulation in Judea when our Lord Jesus walked the earth. He clearly believed that the Old Testament (none of the New Testament had yet been written when our Lord ascended to heaven as described in Acts 1) was the Word of God and not subject to or even on the same plane as other traditions. Our Lord drew this distinction sharply and clearly when He was questioned concerning the washing of hands in Matthew 15 and in Mark 7. Both of these passages are worthy of especially close attention on the question of the authority of the Word of God as opposed to human tradition. Matthew 15:2-3 records the question and our Lord's reply this way:

> *Why do Your disciples transgress the tradition*
> *of the elders? for they wash not their hands*
> *when they eat bread.*
>
> *But He answered and said unto them, Why*
> *do you also transgress the commandment of*
> *God by your tradition?*

Our Lord Jesus then proceeded to denounce the traditional abridgement of the Fifth Commandment to honor our parents. He also said in John 10:35 that the Word of God cannot be broken. This means that the Bible is fundamentally different from any other writing because it is perfect and infallible. Paul in 1 Thessalonians 2:13 phrased this idea this way:

> *For this cause also thank we God without*
> *ceasing, because, when you received the*
> *word of God which you heard from us, you*
> *received it not as the word of men... but as*
> *it is in truth, the word of God, which*
> *effectually works also in you that believe.*

Hebrews 4:12 described the power of the Word of God this way:

> *For the word of God is quick, and powerful,*
> *and sharper than any two-edged sword,*
> *piercing even to the dividing asunder of soul*
> *and spirit, and of the joints and marrow,*
> *and is a discerner of the thoughts and intents*
> *of the heart.*

You may ask what this has to do with abortion. This

principle of the authority of the Word of God over all other sources of argument has application on many topics. But when discussing abortion as well as other issues one frequently hears about a Biblical "tradition" to be weighed against other teachings. No! When a teaching of the Bible has been clearly established, for the faithful Christian that sweeps away all other teachings. The Scriptures are the inspired (literally "God-breathed" in 2 Timothy 3:16) Word of God. Jesus Christ was the Word of God in human flesh. John 1:1. *Forever, O LORD, Your word is settled in heaven.* Psalm 119:89.

With that foundation, we can examine the issue of abortion itself. When does human life begin? David in Psalm 51:5 said that *"Behold, I was shaped in iniquity, and in sin did my mother conceive me."* The presence of sin in David at his conception is a clear indication of life at its very beginning. There is no time when a baby in the womb is not yet human life. Non-living things do not have the property of sin. Both Jeremiah 1:5 and Luke 1:41 show that a baby in the womb was capable of sensing the presence of God. These passages are sufficient to indicate that human life begins at conception and continues through birth. The grief that virtually any woman suffers either from miscarriage or abortion shows that the human conscience understands this intuitively. The ancient Chinese even traditionally viewed a child as being 1 year old at birth.

There is a passage in Exodus 21:22ff. that indirectly confirms this. The main topic deals with a fight between two men. But a pregnant woman apparently tried to appeal to the men to stop and restrain themselves and was jostled in the process. This triggered childbirth, probably prematurely. If there was no loss of life, the consequences would be a fine only. However, if any injury or death occurred to anyone, **including the baby**, that merited additional physical punishment, including death if anyone, **including the baby**, died as a result of the altercation. The baby was regarded as a person in the womb.

While this is not a vital point, a Christian should know that explicit witness to the presence of life in the womb goes all the way back to the *Didache,* which was an instructional manual for Christians in the 2nd century. Abortion was apparently an issue then, because the Christians of those days stood against it. In a truly life-threatening situation such as an ectopic pregnancy where death is inevitable without medical intervention, Scriptural principals do not require that we stand by and watch the mother die. This is a matter of self-defense, even though the misplaced baby does not know the havoc that he or she is causing. But even in cases such as this, Christian principles would require that the baby be put in an artificial womb and nurtured if this is possible in order to spare his or her life in the process of sparing the mother. The *Didache* is not inspired Scripture, but it is historical evidence of a standard of conduct maintained by Christians through the centuries. Our witness for the presence of human life from conception forward is part the unity of Christian doctrine and fellowship across the centuries among all who have loved and obeyed the Scriptures.

CHAPTER 6
Biblical Teaching: Divorce

As marriage was created by God originally in Genesis 2, divorce was not even discussed because there was at that time no sin. In general, there is a large gulf between Christianity and the 21st century secularist world concerning marriage. Is it a human device that we are free to define and restructure as we may think best? Advocates of same-sex marriage and of "divorce for any cause" (as phrased in the question of Matthew 19) apparently think so. Or is marriage a divine treasure committed to our safekeeping for future generations? If so, we are free to receive the gift of marriage but not to make fundamental changes in its divine design. We have already discussed polygamy. We will reserve the issues of same-sex marriage for future discussion and focus on divorce first.

After sin and death entered the world so that all human beings became subject to physical death, marriages could at any time be severed by death. But what if clashes between husband and wife made the home unpleasant or even worse? When God gave the Law to Israel, He knew that the Law would have to govern relationships among stubborn people who were not necessarily committed to God Himself nor to either of the greatest commandments of the Law:

1) *You shall love the Lord your God with all your heart, with all your soul, with all your mind and with all your strength;* (Deuteronomy 6:5 as expanded in Mark 12:30) and

2) *You shall love your neighbor as yourself.* (Leviticus 19:18; Mark 12:31)

Therefore Moses indeed permitted divorce for "uncleanness" in Deuteronomy 24:1-4. Moses did require a written statement of the divorce, which would legally free both parties to marry again. But Moses did not elaborate on the requirement of "uncleanness." Some rabbinical speculation stretched this word so far as to include a displeasing meal. Virtually any imperfection would serve as grounds of divorce in the eyes of some (though not all) schools of rabbinical thought. So when the time came for Jesus Christ to be tested mentally and morally before taking our sins upon Himself as the Lamb of God, the question of divorce was put to Him in Matthew 19:1-10. As we noted before, our Lord Jesus first placed marriage back on its original Creation foundation and then taught concerning divorce from this Biblical foundation. Then Matthew 5:31-32, Matthew 19:1-10, Mark 10:1-12 and Luke 16:18 record our Lord's teaching. Mark and Luke emphasize the basic principle that marriages are in principle not to be dissolved while both partners live. Matthew gives the fullest account and records the one exception that our Lord gave: adultery by one of the parties. It should be recalled that under Moses' Law adultery was a crime to be punished by the death penalty. In a world where this Law were enforced, divorce on the basis of adultery would not be necessary because the adulterer (if so proved by legal proof by at least 2 witnesses) would be executed. But this was not done in Jesus' time -- in fact, the Jewish government had lost completely the power to order or carry out a death sentence for any reason. (John 18:31) This could only be done by the Roman governor, as in the case of our Lord Jesus Himself. The Roman aristocracy viewed adultery as a routine part of life. Therefore our Lord Jesus did permit divorce upon proof of adultery as a practical adjustment to imperfect human government. He knew, as so many of his His contemporaries did not, the suffering of a spouse innocent of this sin and also the danger of disease transmission. In the light of modern knowledge of sexually transmitted diseases, how true are the words of the Apostle Paul in 1 Corinthians 6:18! *Flee fornication. Every sin that a man does is ouside the body; but he that commits fornication sins against his own body.*

The Apostle Paul dealt with additional issues concerning divorce in 1 Corinthians 7. Paul does not deal with the subject of adultery in this chapter -- that had already been taught by Jesus Christ. Paul was dealing with problems which arose when a married person who had married before his or her conversion then was saved through the Lord Jesus Christ. What then to make of the marriage and of the children of that marriage? Paul taught that the newly saved person should remain in the marriage if the other partner were also willing to continue the marriage. The newly saved partner should also stay with the children, if any. There should be no concerns of any ceremonial uncleanness of other family members, even when dealing with the most intimate bodily contact between husband and wife. Paul's essential command was to stay with the marriage if possible. If the other partner refused to tolerate the convert's Christianity and consequently refused to live in peace with the convert, then the convert should let the other person leave. In such a case the new convert was not bound to the marriage and could divorce and remarry. This was an issue which arose primarily among the Gentiles to whom Paul preached rather than within Israel. However, there are no other circumstances in which the New Testament permits divorce among the people of God. (This is a different question from how Deuteronomy 24 should be understood by the modern legislator in governing people who are predominantly rebellious against God. Deuteronomy 24 is still God's inspired Word in dealing with a community composed of people with no real love for God. Matthew 19 says that Moses permitted divorce "because of the hardness of your hearts." That standard appears to be more permissive than the standard set by the Lord Jesus, judging from His own words. We do not need to explore the legislator's dilemma further for now.)

Once divorced, can a person remarry? Under Moses' code, the answer was clearly yes. But we must consider what our Lord Jesus said, *Whosoever puts away his wife, except it be for the cause of adultery, commits adultery; and whosoever marries her who is divorced commits adultery.*

Matthew 19:9. Taking the verse as a whole, it is clear that a person who has been validly divorced because of his or her adultery cannot remarry with the approval of God. If a person does obtain a divorce for the other spouse's adultery, there is nothing in the verse that forbids remarriage in that situation if the adultery charge is indeed true.

The question of remarriage after divorce is also mentioned in 1 Corinthians 7:15: *If the unbelieving depart, let him depart. A brother or a sister is not under bondage in such cases: but God hath called us to peace.* Taking the phrase "not under bondage" straightforwardly, it would appear that the deserted partner can remarry after the divorce. We see the same phrase in English in Romans 7:2 in stating that a woman is "bound to the law of her husband." When I examine the Greek lexicon, the two words translated are not precisely the same, but the Greek scholars think that the words are synonymous. Thus one is bound to a willing spouse but not to a spouse who insists on breaking up the marriage because of the salvation of the other partner. In the latter case a deserted and divorced spouse may remarry as a spouse who has obtained a divorce as a result of adultery by his or her former spouse.

Ephesians 5:22-33 likens the relationship between Christ and His Church with the relationship between husband and wife. We know from Matthew 28:19-20, from the last chapters of Revelation and from many other passages that the relationship between Christ and the Church will never be broken. When a divorce occurs, especially between professing Christians, the analogy has been violated and a spiritual lie is being fed to the community because of the implication that the relationship between Christ and His Bride, the true Church, can be broken when in fact it cannot. This lie may be part of the reason why 1 Timothy 3 and Titus 1 appear to prohibit a divorced man from serving as a deacon or elder without distinction as to the reason for the divorce; the other reason is for the sake of the reputation of the church to the outside community.

When one enters into marriage, one is making a lifetime commitment to God and to the other person to form a marriage that will last for life.

[If you desire further discussion at this point of the "legislator's dilemma" about divorce and other subjects mentioned in this chapter, go to Appendix B on this topic. For further discussion on the practical impact of holiness as an integral part of any individual Christian's life, read Appendix C.]

CHAPTER 7

Biblical Teaching: Adultery & Same-Sex Marriage Plus A Thumbnail Sketch Of The Afterlife

If polls are to be believed, sexual purity is rare today. Certainly the spread of sexually transmitted diseases indicates a grave moral and medical problem. *Newsmax Magazine* reports that 40% of American children are born to mothers who are not married. Political careers of leaders of both major American political parties have been wrecked by sexual unfaithfulness. Even common experience teaches us that breaking up intimate relationships gives great psychological stress to the partners.

What does the Bible teach about adultery? We know that it is forbidden by the Seventh Commandment. Adultery occurs when one or both of the participants in sexual intimacy are married to a person other than their current sexual partner. Under Moses' Law, adultery if proved meant the death penalty for the offenders, both male and female. Leviticus 20:10. The Law makes it clear that where intercourse occurs between two people who both are unmarried, that this is not the capital crime of adultery but is nevertheless regarded so seriously that marriage should be normal result. Exodus 22:16. The Apostle Paul uses the term "one flesh", normally used of marriage, even of a relationship to a prostitute. 1 Corinthians 6:15-16.

It should be noted that in addition to the physical diseases often associated with adultery and other forms of indiscriminate sexual relations that nations that practice these things have been judged. In Jeremiah's time it was written of Jerusalem's prophets (23:14),

> I have seen also in the prophets of Jerusalem
> a horrible thing: they commit adultery, and
> walk in lies: they strengthen also the hands
> of evildoers, that none does return from his
> wickedness: they are all of them unto me as
> Sodom, and the inhabitants thereof as
> Gomorrah.

Not long after these words were written, Jerusalem was burnt and leveled to the ground by Nebuchadnezzar of Babylon.

What happened to Sodom and Gomorrah? What does the Bible teach about homosexuality and same-sex marriages? Since the Bible is God's Word to humanity, we cannot ignore the answer because it runs against the fashion of our times. Genesis 18 and 19 give the basic answer. Abraham prayed for Sodom and Gomorrah; God eventually told Abraham that he would spare them if there were as many as 10 righteous men there. In fact there was only one: Lot, Abraham's nephew (2 Peter 2:7). Even Lot was compromised by his desire for wealth and comfort when he chose to live in the area of Sodom when he and Abraham parted, but he had enough sense to take the two "men" (actually the Angel of the Lord -- a pre-birth form of the Son of God -- and another angel disguised as men) inside his house rather than leave them to the men of the city. When men of the city found out that there were two foreign males in Lot's house, they demanded that Lot bring them out for their homosexual gratification and threatened to storm his house if they refused. Lot offered them his daughters instead, but the men in the crowd were not interested. This reaction confirmed God's disgust with the inhabitants of the region expressed to Abraham. At dawn the two angels led Lot and his family out of the city and showered fatal fire and brimstone on the region, exterminating the population and making a prosperous land a waste. The region, which is south and east of the Dead Sea, is still uninhabitable even after the passage of about 4000 years.

So what does God think of same-sex sexual relationships? By His actions He has demonstrated that He hates them! By the same token, He also hates adulterous male-female relationships as shown by the passage already quoted in Jeremiah saying that the adulterous prophets were like Sodom and Gomorrah. God has not left us to draw the lesson by physical object lesson alone. He has reaffirmed his graphic warnings about same-sex relationships in several passages in the New Testament:

Wherefore God also gave them up to uncleanness through the lusts of their own hearts, to dishonor their own bodies between themselves, who changed the truth of God into a lie, and worshipped and served the creature more than the Creator, who is blessed for ever. Amen.

For this cause God gave them up unto vile affections, for even their women did change the natural use into that which is against nature. And likewise also the men, leaving the natural use of the woman, burned in their lust one toward another; men with men working that which is unseemly, and receiving in themselves that recompense of their error which was just.

And even as they did not like to retain God in their knowledge, God gave them over to a reprobate mind, to do those things which are not convenient: being filled with all unrighteousness, fornication, wickedness, covetousness, maliciousness; full of envy, murder, debate, deceit, malignity; whisperers, backbiters, haters of God, despiteful, proud, boasters, inventors of evil things, disobedient to parents,

Without understanding, covenantbreakers, without natural affection, implacable, unmerciful: Who knowing the judgment of

> *God, that they which commit such things*
> *are worthy of death, not only do the same,*
> *but have pleasure in them that do them.*

This is a quotation of Romans 1:24-32 with a change of one outdated word ("just" is substituted for "meet" used in the now archaic sense of "fitting"). Not all the things that mankind may do to anger God are sexual in nature, but misuse of God's gift of sexuality outside of marriage between one man and one woman is certainly prominent in this extensive list of things that anger God and provoke Him to judgmental action. As concerning most of our entertainment industry, notice the condemnation of taking "pleasure in them that do [these things]." God is displeased if we enjoy evil in others even if we stop short of doing it ourselves. If our nation were using an accurate moral compass, the marketplace itself would clean up much of the wickedness in our mass media because the makers would lose money.

As further confirmation, we read in 1 Corinthians 6:9-11 that:

> *Don't you know that the unrighteous shall*
> *not inherit the kingdom of God? Do not be*
> *deceived: neither fornicators, nor idolaters,*
> *nor adulterers, nor effeminate, nor abusers*
> *of themselves with mankind, nor thieves,*
> *nor covetous, nor drunkards, nor revilers,*
> *nor extortioners, shall inherit the kingdom*
> *of God. And such **were** some of you: but*
> *you **are** washed, but you **are** sanctified, but*
> *you **are** justified in the name of the Lord*
> *Jesus, and by the Spirit of our God.*

I have emphasized the verbs to make it easy to see their tense, which is crucial. There is an enormous difference between what the believers ***were*** and what they ***are***. God's Spirit has drawn all kinds of people into God's Kingdom, including those who had had the worst characters and had practiced the worst vices. This passage does not specifically mention murder, but Paul described himself as the chief of sinners (1 Timothy 1:15), probably remembering that he was a principal in the second degree in Stephen's murder (Acts 6-9) by holding the coats of the actual killers and then his later persecutions of the Church. As Paul's character was changed drastically, so were the characters of the former "low-lifes" who had been transformed from the inside out to become part of the Christian church in Corinth.

Should we then hate sinners or even take the law into our own hands and kill them because their deeds and character are hateful to God? No! We started the same way, whatever our individual characteristics may have been. Pride is also hateful to God. For example see Proverbs 6:17; 16:5; 21:4; 28:25. This same type of debate has arisen over snipers who have aimed at abortionists. The Holy Scriptures are plain that as private citizens we are not to take to ourselves the place of judge, jury and executioner. Romans 12:19 states,

> *Dearly beloved, avenge not yourselves, but rather give place unto wrath: for it is written, Vengeance is mine; I will repay, saith the Lord.*

Romans 3:5-8 also forbids evil means, such as hate and murder, to achieve good ends. The time, place and method of vengeance is to be determined by God, not by us. Further, some of the people that we may be inclined to hate the most may be chosen by God for dramatic transformation. While we cannot approve deeds of wickedness, we are still to pray for and to seek to call all sorts of sinners to the same repentance that God so graciously granted to us.

A THUMBNAIL SKETCH OF THE AFTERLIFE

At this point we should examine another issue that is not directly connected with family life but has a profound impact on all of Christian ethics. What is the afterlife? Are heaven and the Lake of Fire real? All of Christianity is premised on the reality of the resurrection. Paul in 1 Corinthians 15:13-19 addresses this extensively, ending with this conclusion, *"If in this life only we have hope in Christ, we are of all men most miserable."* Conversely, when God speaks of vengeance as he executed upon Sodom, was this only for this life? Jude 7 says this,

> *Even as Sodom and Gomorrah, and the cities about them in like manner, giving themselves over to fornication, and going after strange flesh, are set forth for an example, suffering the vengeance of* <u>*eternal fire.*</u> *(emphasis added)*

This passage is teaching that the vengeance on Sodom and Gomorrah did not stop when the embers of the fire on earth went out, but that the fire continues to today and beyond. Why study such a severe subject?

1) To be more grateful for the grace of God by better understanding our extreme degree of natural guilt and the just penalty of our sin;

2) To motivate us to be faithful witnesses. If Christians

remain silent as to their faith, what awaits their friends, acquaintences and even their enemies? (*Love your enemies ...* Matthew 5:44) Consider the Christian's responsibility as a watchman, *But if the watchman see the sword come, and blow not the trumpet, and the people be not warned; if the sword come, and take any person from among them, he is taken away in his iniquity; but his blood will I require at the watchman's hand.* Ezekiel 33:6;

3) To better understand the holiness of God by better understanding His righteous indignation against sin, especially deliberate sin. If we understand better God's ultimate punishment, it will be easier to obey God's command to stay out of His way and let His wrath operate instead of our own puny power if He does not choose mercy. (Albert Speer wrote that a German general who apparently believed in God persuaded Speer to stop trying to assassinate Hitler based on this reasoning near the end of World War 2. Hitler killed himself not long after that.);

4) To better understand why the sufferings of Jesus Christ on the Cross had to be so gruesome to complete the payment for our sin;

5) To motivate ourselves to be more holy by considering the character of God as expressed in both His love and His vengeance (Romans 11:22);

6) To spur us to prayer for the lost, considering what is truly at stake for eternity;

7) To understand within the limitations of our humanity what our Lord Jesus meant when He spoke of "hellfire"

(Matthew 5:22) and equivalent expressions such as Mark 9:43-48;

8) To understand better and to give thanks better for the contrast between our country of ultimate citizenship in heaven and the final wrath of God in the Lake of Fire;

9) To stimulate and renew within us the proper fear of God, which is the beginning of wisdom; and

10) To more fully understand the unsearchable riches of Christ (such as salvation, heaven itself, the rewards we are graciously permitted to seek, etc.) by contrasting them as jewels against the black background of the everlasting punishment that we deserve by nature.

11) To bear adversity or injustice without bitterness or despair, knowing that nothing that can happen on earth is even comparable to what we truly deserve from God were it not for the saving blood-sacrifice of Jesus Christ.

I have not come close to exhausting the reasons why we need to study this, but this should be enough to go forward. These reasons are not stated in a particular order.

Jude starting in verse 6 compared false teachers to angels *"who did not keep their first estate."* Apparently some of these roam the earth as demons and others have been confined in total darkness by God until the Day of Judgment. These angels are condemned to everlasting darkness. Our Lord Jesus in Matthew 25:30 spoke of the unprofitable servant being cast into "outer darkness"; in Matthew 25:41 He stated that wicked humanity would be thrown into fire "prepared for the devil and his angels."

So unsaved humanity, Satan and the fallen angels will have a common everlasting punishment. Luke 16:19-31 gives a picture of an unsaved man after physical death, showing that the torment is real. That rich man was in a temporary holding place before the final Lake of Fire, but the portrait does give us a glimpse of the Final Judgment. The main elements shown are heat, thirst and darkness. (As a comparison, our Lord Jesus specifically said *"I thirst"* on the Cross as part of His bearing our sin. John 19:28)

There is another clue from the contrast of Jude 13 when compared to Job 38:7. The false teachers (perhaps demonic and human) are called "wandering stars" while the angels in right relation to God are called "morning stars" in Job. From this I draw the inference that stars in general represent angels or at least have some connection to angels. As a corollary I think that the phrase that the *"stars in their courses fought against Sisera"* (Judges 5:20) is a reference to angelic intervention in favor of Deborah and Barak and of all Israel. It might be that stars are physical representations of holy angels.

The <u>History Channel</u> had an interesting explanation of "black holes" that are now known to exist in outer space. These are said to swallow and destroy stars, and they have several properties that would fit the Biblical description of judgment. Their gravitational force is so intense that not even light can escape. Surely any living creature which falls into a black hole would be imprisoned there permanently and probably could not even move any part of its body. Their darkness fits Jude's description. Despite the darkness, they are so hot that even a fire on earth is cool by comparison.

Were a human being sucked into a black hole by its

overpowering gravity, he or she would be crushed instantly. Since the back and the rest of the skeleton would be crushed in the process, the pain in the back alone would be excruciating. All spinal discs would be herniated. One can only image the impact of the supergravity on bodily fluids in the stomach and eyes. Since we know that the moon's gravity influences tides even of great oceans, the gravitational pull on bodily fluids would be beyond description. One cannot imagine the effect on the teeth and the sensitive nerves there. I do not claim that my inferences are an exact scientific description of what the Lake of Fire would be like. But this is based on the partial description that God has given us in the Bible -- His Word is telling us in terms of the present known world that the pain of the Lake of Fire is something like this, even if caused differently in the world to come. The body involved may be virtual and the pain may be similar to the phantom pain that an amputee may sense from a severed limb, but the pain is real, ruthless and relentless.

And this is not all. The fire that fell on Sodom and Gomorrah was brimstone, which means that it contained burning sulfur. From high school chemistry we know that sulfur compounds in the atmosphere, such as hydrogen sulfide ("rotten eggs"), sulfur dioxide or gaseous sulfuric acid are noxious and cause extreme discomfort to the lungs and stomach. When one considers that the sulfurous atmosphere would be superheated, the lungs and other organs would be seared internally in addition to the nausea in the Lake of Fire. The skin would also be burned on the outside. The pain that we know from sunburn would not even touch the pain caused by the total burns of the entire skin (or equivalent) in a black hole or the final Lake of Fire.

Revelation 14:10 tells us that all who receive the mark of the Beast shall drink the wrath of God. This portrays a punishment to the internal digestive organs of the body. I infer from this combined with the sulfurous atmosphere that part of the punishment will be a sensation of perpetual hiccups, retching and gagging in addition to the burning heat.

The odor of the Lake of Fire, having burning sulfur and burning flesh among its components, can only be sickening beyond comprehension or description.

Complete darkness was a form of torture used by the North Vietnamese on some of the bravest of American flyers such as Jeremiah Denton, who entitled his book about his prison experiences <u>When Hell Was In Session.</u> He later became a Senator from Alabama. John McCain, Robbie Risner and David Stockdale, among others, also suffered greatly as prisoners. No mere human being has a right to inflict such torture on another; but God does have the right to so punish those of rebel against Him. In the Lake of Fire, the darkness will be perpetual and complete. Egypt suffered the judgment of darkness so gross that it was painful for a few days as part of the breaking of Pharaoh's grip to force him to let Israel go. Exodus 10:21. In the Lake of Fire such darkness will be perpetual. In Sodom the same effect was achieved by blinding the people.

The pain in the Lake of Fire is not confined to the physical. The rich man of Luke 16:19-31 was told by Abraham to *"Remember that you in your lifetime received good things ..."* So the damned can remember. What a contrast between earth and the Lake of Fire! The condemned probably can also remember how they led others (family and friends, for example) away from the truth and the responsibility he or she may bear for their suffering.

There will be no rest nor sleep. Revelation 20:10 speaks directly about the unholy trinity of Satan, the Beast and the False Prophet, but it seems clear that all unbelievers share their punishment. There shall be no painkillers, not even aspirin. There will be no water -- the heat would vaporize it anyway. Perhaps worst of all, there will be no mercy from God and no love will exist in the Lake of Fire. The last of God's patience has been exhausted. Even allowing for the fact that the Greek Bible speaks of three kinds of love, there obviously can be no erotic love in such an environment when one person cannot even see another. There can be no brotherly fellowship for the same reason and for the additional reason that the suffering will be so intense that each denizen of the Lake of Fire will be pre-occupied with himself or herself. There can be no sacrificial love (*agape*) because the sacrifice of Christ which is its highest expression has been rejected.

No wonder our Lord Jesus described this as a place of *"weeping, wailing and gnashing of teeth."* I am unsure whether the sounds will be smothered entirely by the gravity and atmosphere or whether everyone will hear everyone else's screaming, but surely there will be no joy or comfort. We naturally recoil from such awful punishment, but we have to remember that offenses against God are offenses against a Person Who is infinitely good, righteous and powerful. The majesty of the offended party magnifies the offense. In the military, a private slapping a general would be handled differently from a general slapping a private. An assault by one co-worker against another, however wrong, is treated differently from an assault of the same force against the Queen of England or the President of the United States. So offenses against an infinite God require in justice an infinite punishment, which I have tried to describe as closely as I can. I know that given my imperfection that I will be wide of the mark in some ways and that especially I will be short of the mark. My description is too mild. But if this gets our thinking closer to God's truth than it was before, it is worthwhile.

There is still another aspect of the Lake of Fire. Those punished there will be the target of divine sarcasm. *He that dwells in the heavens shall laugh; the Lord shall have them in derision. Then shall He speak to them in His wrath, and vex them in His severe displeasure.* Psalm 2:4-5. It would be no joke to hear the perpetual rebuke of the Almighty or to be the target of His sarcastic humor.

In contrast, let us consider heaven as well. As there will be no day in the Lake of Fire, there will be no night in heaven. Revelation 22:5. The light will be supplied by the risen Lord Jesus. Revelation in several passages (5:8, for example) makes it clear that the sound of music beyond that of earth resounds in heaven. Water is abundant (7:17, 22:1). There will be no crying there (Rev. 7:16-17). There will be no unpleasant heat in heaven. Our bodies, instead of being wracked with pain, shall be like the glorious resurrection body of our Lord Jesus Christ. 1 Corinthians 15:42-44; Philippians 3:21. There will be no need for painkillers because there will be no more pain nor tears from either physical or emotional causes. Revelation 21:4. While the wicked in the Lake of Fire are perpetually reminded of their transgressions, the righteous have all of theirs washed away and forgotten. *As far as the east is from the west, so far has He removed our transgressions from us.* Psalm 103:12. While the wicked are cast away from Him, those whom He has made righteous are taken up to Him. Instead of rebuke, the faithful hear this, *Enter into the joy of your Lord.* Matthew 25:21, 23.

While there is no freedom of movement in the Lake of Fire, there is infinite freedom of movement to the citizen of heaven. Philippians 3:21 reminds us that our resurrection body will be like Jesus' glorious resurrection body. Jesus Christ in His resurrected state was able to move between earth and heaven freely (Acts 1) and was able to enter a room without using the door (Luke 24:36). Even before His death, there was a hint of such a power in John 6:21, where our Lord not only had just walked on water but was able to transport the boat and the disciples instantly to land. Our bodies, like His, will be able to exceed the speed of light. I believe that the citizen of heaven will have the ability (like a multitasking computer in this respect) to be present at multiple places at one time and to worship the Father, Son and Spirit in multiple ways at once. This is a fair inference of the words, *We shall be like Him, for we shall see Him as He is.* 1 John 3:2. Philippians 3:21 also supports this idea.

In contrast to the odors of the Lake of Fire, the odors of heaven are wonderful. Incense is among them. Revelation 8:3-4. The Tree of Life of Revelation 22 likely contributes another fragrant odor of joy. I can barely begin to guess at the totality of the glories of heaven, for *Eye hath not seen, nor ear heard, neither have entered into the heart of man, the things which God hath prepared for them that love him.* 1 Corinthians 2:9, based on Isaiah 64:4.

Love will be superabundant in heaven, because God is always present. While there will be no need for erotic love (Matthew 22:30), we will be taken up constantly with joy and fellowship and we will benefit continuously without end from the self-sacrificing love of the Savior. We shall love Him fully in return. The curse of the Garden of Eden will finally be reversed. As Isaiah wrote (51:11):

> *Therefore the redeemed of the LORD shall return, and come with singing unto Zion; and everlasting joy shall be upon their head: they shall obtain gladness and joy; and sorrow and mourning shall flee away.*

This is only a small part of the blessings of heaven, but surely this shows the blessedness of the people of God. Unbelief and consequent disobedience will lead to the Lake of Fire. Saving faith, which generates obedience, will lead to everlasting life because God in His grace wills it to be so.

IN THE LIGHT OF THE AFTERLIFE, HOW SHOULD WE LIVE NOW?

What choices concerning sexuality does a teenager or older person have if he or she desires to obey God? According to Matthew 19:1-10 and 1 Corinthians 7, there are two: faithfulness in a monogamous marriage to a person of the opposite sex or celibacy, which means the absence of any sexual relations. For those who can handle it, celibacy is prized highly because it frees up more time for the direct service of God. However, there are few adults that can endure a truly celibate life, which involves a complete avoidance of sexual expression and a mind disciplined enough to suppress sexual temptation without even dwelling on the thought, let alone the act. As the Lord Jesus taught, *"For whosoever has lusted after a woman has already committed adultery with her in his heart."* Matthew 5:28

As holiness is mandatory in all portions of life, sexual holiness is mandatory for the true believer. A professing Christian who continues to practice by habit any form of sexual deviation from God's standard may well be a counterfeit rather than a real believer. We have already mentioned 1 Corinthians 6:9-10, which reads:

> *Don't you know that the unrighteous shall not inherit the kingdom of God? Be not deceived: neither fornicators, nor idolaters, nor adulterers, nor effeminate, nor abusers of themselves with mankind, nor thieves, nor covetous, nor drunkards, nor revilers, nor extortioners, shall inherit the kingdom of God.*

The next verse deals with the Christian's transformation from a person who used to enjoy such things. Consider also Revelation 22:14-15, which says:

> *Blessed are they that do His commandments, that they may have right to the tree of life, and may enter in through the gates into the city. For outside are dogs, and sorcerers,*

> and whoremongers, and murderers, and
> idolaters, and whosoever loves and makes a
> lie.

Hebrews 12:14 commands us to *"Follow peace with all, and holiness, without which no man shall see the Lord."* James (2:18) challenges us to *"Show me your faith without your works, and I will show you my faith by my works.* This passage returns us to the truth that faith that is solely intellectual is dead and not true, living faith. 2 Corinthians 5:17 tells us that any person in Christ is a new creation -- the old has passed away. Romans 6 and Romans 8 likewise teach that the original person has died with conversion and that there is a new person rising from the dead. So it is quite possible that some of the worst people ever may be redeemed through the saving power of Jesus Christ, but it is not possible that such a person will remain after salvation the same as he or she was before. Complete escape from the power of the grossest sin is not always instantaneous, but with time the power of the Holy Spirit shows through a transformed inner character and a new behavior that corresponds to the new inner man. While we will never be perfect in this life, we will become sufficiently holy given time that we will be readily distinguishable from most of the world.

[For further discussion of the judgment from the standpoint of the character of God, see Appendix D. For further discussion of the judgment from the standpoint of justice, see Appendix E.]

Chapter 8

The Necessity Of Holiness & The Last Judgment

Our previous study of some of the contrasts between Heaven and the Lake of Fire might be summarized in tabular form like this:

	Heaven	Lake of Fire
Light	All light, no darkness or night	All darkness, no light
Freedom	Can exceed speed of light	No movement; crushing gravity
Pain	None	Excruciating
Crying, grief	None	Constant
Fellowship	Constant without end	None

God's greeting	Commendation and welcome	Sarcasm and condemnation
Smells	Incense and other pleasant odors	Sulfur, burning flesh, etc.
Past memories	Sins forgotten forever	Sins remembered forever
Water	Abundant	None
Music	Glorious; joyous	None; possible wailing, etc.
Our sounds	Praise and worship	Screams, curses, weeping, wailing,
Love	Infinite love all the time	No love forever

Every human being of understanding should live his or her entire life with at least one eye on eternity. All seven of the letters of our Lord Jesus Christ in Revelation 2 & 3 make some reference to the Last Judgment or to the afterlife that follows the Last Judgment. Our every word is subject to re-examination at the Judgment. Matthew 12:36. Before we do anything of significance, we should ask ourselves the question: How will this look on Instant Replay? Revelation 20:12-13.

So many prominent people imagine that they can somehow get away with sin. If other men and women don't know, who cares? God! As Ezekiel (9:9) wrote:

> *Then said He unto me, "The iniquity of the house of Israel and Judah is exceedingly*

> *great, and the land is full of blood, and the*
> *city full of perverseness: for they say, 'The*
> *LORD has forsaken the earth, and the*
> *LORD sees not.'"*

Moses warned in Numbers 32:23, *Be sure your sin will find you out.* So many times this happens to our shame while we are still on the earth, but this is actually a door for mercy. It is better to have shame before men drive us to repentance than for us to deceive ourselves that we have hidden our sins successfully, only to have Jesus Himself condemn us at the Day of Judgment. Far better still to confess our sinful natures before Jesus Christ before they have expressed themselves fully and asked for His forgiveness and the changing power of the Holy Spirit before sin has run its full course. As James says (1:15), *Then when lust has conceived, it brings forth sin: and sin, when it is finished, brings forth death.* James 4:6-10 also summarizes the remedy:

> *But He gives more grace. Wherefore He says,*
> *God resists the proud, but gives grace unto*
> *the humble. Submit yourselves therefore to*
> *God. Resist the devil, and he will flee from*
> *you. Draw near to God, and He will draw*
> *near to you. Cleanse your hands, you sinners;*
> *and purify your hearts, you double-minded.*
> *Be afflicted, and mourn, and weep: let your*
> *laughter be turned to mourning, and your*
> *joy to heaviness. Humble yourselves in the*
> *sight of the Lord, and He shall lift you up.*

As Paul said in the immediate context of the Lord's Supper, *If we would judge ourselves, we should not be judged.* 1 Corinthians 11:31.

Hebrews 9:27 says simply that *"it is appointed to men once to die, and after this the judgment."* Peter makes unmistakably clear that all individuals will have to account to God for their words and actions. He spoke specifically of pagans *"who shall give account to Him that is ready to judge the living and the dead."* 1 Peter 4:5. Jude 14-15 expands on this, saying:

> *And Enoch also, the seventh from Adam, prophesied of these, saying, Behold, the Lord comes with ten thousands of his saints, to execute judgment upon all, and to convict all that are ungodly among them of all their ungodly deeds which they have ungodly committed, and of all their hard speeches which ungodly sinners have spoken against Him.*

When coupled with the Sermon on the Mount (Matthew 5-7) with its emphasis that even one sinful thought is enough to be guilty of the substantive offense (Matthew 5:21-22 in the case of murder and 5:27-30 in the case of adultery, for example and also note Hebrews 4:12), we can readily discern three things:

A) The absolute necessity of divine forgiveness to survive the Judgment;

B) The importance of internal purity to receive commendation in the Judgment; and

C) The importance of good works (for example, Matthew 25:31-46 and James 2:14-18) as evidence of true faith to receive commendation in the Judgment.

So then it is important to consider the Judgment in more detail. The Scriptures mention a judgment for believers only in 2 Corinthians 5:10, which concerns the rewards or failures of the believer as a faithful steward of God. This is also described in 1 Corinthians 3:10-15 in terms of the building materials we have used to build on the foundation, Christ Jesus. The faithful stewards of Matthew 25:15-23 also received rewards. God has through His grace permitted us to enter a rewards program which we do not deserve and cannot earn to stir us up to good works. Participate in the program with vigor and diligence.

The climax of all truth concerning the Last Judgment is that where the saved and the unsaved, the sheep and the goats, are brought together as described in Matthew 25:31-46. First consider the Judge, Jesus Christ. The most detailed portrait of Him after His resurrection is found in Revelation 1, when He appeared to John. In Daniel, the resurrected Son of God is referred to as the Ancient of Days, and so Revelation 1:14 describes His head and hair as white, like that of an old patriarch who retains his vigor. But His eyes are anything but old -- they burn with fire. His feet shine like brass -- we are familiar with shined trumpets and cornets in a band. His voice sounds like a waterfall. If any of you have hear Niagara Falls between Canada and the United States, the roar of the falls would be a comparison to the strength of His voice. The sword coming out of His mouth (compare Hebrews 4:12 again) indicates that the risen Lord Jesus needs no human weapons to fight His war -- His words alone can and do kill and punish forever. His nature as the Light of the World (John 1:9) is reflected in His face, which shines like the Sun. John, the most intimate and beloved of all the Apostles, here fell at Jesus' feet as if dead. The risen Jesus Christ can rivet attention to Himself and control a crowd by Himself as no politician ever could. When He will be present at the Judgment, He will be able to rivet attention and impose order without any help.

The angels, far stronger in physical force than human beings although inferior to Jesus Christ, will also be present at the judgment. They have already done their work in separating the wheat from the tares (Matthew 13); in Matthew 25:31-46 the sheep (followers) and the goats (resisters) have already been separated into two sections. If bailiffs were necessary, the loyal angels would be ideal bailiffs at the Last Judgment, with ample power to enforce order and to silence protesters. However, this will probably not be necessary because the mere presence of the risen Jesus Christ is more than sufficient to maintain order.

In human criminal courtrooms, both the prosecutor and the defense counsel portray aspects of the Last Judgment although most do not think about it often. The Law, sometimes personnified as Moses, the man who gave the Law to Israel, is the accuser and prosecutor. John 1:17; John 5:45-46. (Satan is the Accuser of the Brethren -- Revelation 12:10 -- but Satan's accusations are legally false because the Law has been blotted out for believers through the blood sacrifice of the Lamb of God which has already paid our penalty. Colossians 2:13-14. Therefore Satan can no longer accuse us before God in the manner in which he accused Job. Hallelujah!) The Lord Jesus Himself is our defense counsel; in 1 John 2:1 that is the meaning of "Advocate."

> *My little children, these things write I unto*
> *you, that you sin not. And if any man sin,*
> *we have an Advocate with the Father, Jesus*
> *Christ the righteous. And He is the*
> *propitiation for our sins: and not for ours*
> *only, but also for the sins of the whole world.*
> *1 John 2:1-2.*

This is one reason why the faithful can be so confident about their acquittal on Judgment Day. Contrary to any human courtroom, the Judge is also their Lawyer! We do not earn an acquittal on our own, it is given to us because the sacrifice of Jesus Christ has satisfied God's demand for justice in our cases. Our Lawyer has paid with His human life for our acquittal.

As an afterword, I plead once more as a pardoned spiritual criminal myself to you to repent of your sins and trust in the Lord Jesus Christ. He Himself posed the question, *"You serpents, you generation of vipers, how can you escape the damnation of hell?* Matthew 23:33. Similar Biblical indictments can be found in Matthew 3:7, Luke 3:7 and Matthew 12:34. God calls us all snakes! We react in our minds: HOW DARE HE ACCUSE ME? But the accusation is true and just. If we are honest with ourselves we will at least privately admit it. It is we who are dead wrong. If you have any doubt of this, read Romans 3:9-18 and Romans 6:23 again. I have not overdone the human reaction to God's blunt assessment of human nature. Consider Romans 9:18-23. Consider how puny we all are compared to the Lord Jesus as portrayed in Revelation 1.

Those who do not trust Jesus Christ for their salvation

have cut themselves off from their only hope. To them our Lord Jesus will speak the terrible words recorded in Matthew 7:23, *"I never knew you: depart from me, you that work iniquity."* That departure is to the terrible conscious perpetual death summarized in our table and sketched in a bit more detail when we examined the necessity of holiness and purity. Many in Peter's first audience realized that they and the leadership of Israel were guilty of murder in the crucifixion of the Lord Jesus. They cried out: *Men and brethren, what shall we do?* Acts 2:37. I relay Peter's answer as my close:

> *Then Peter said unto them, "Repent, and be baptized every one of you in the name of Jesus Christ for the remission of sins, and ye shall receive the gift of the Holy Spirit. For the promise is unto you, and to your children, and to all that are afar off, even as many as the Lord our God shall call."*
>
> *And with many other words did he testify and exhort, saying, "Save yourselves from this crooked generation." Then they that gladly received his word were baptized: and the same day there were added unto them about three thousand souls. Acts 2:38-41.*

Appendix A

Earned Salvation? Never!

It is a common teaching that a person will have to pay for his or her sins by fiery suffering after death, and then after a time of suffering enter heaven. This doctrine appeals to our human sense of justice and also to our innate desire to earn our own way to God's presence. Sin is minimized falsely to the point that we can pay for it, given enough time and heroism or stoicism. But this doctrine also misrepresents God and cuts short the true glory of Jesus Christ.

Other religions have the idea that we may be reincarnated again as a human or as a lesser being, such as a fly or an animal. The concept is that eventually we may accumulate enough wisdom or merit to enter *nirvana,* a utopian state. While the mechanism is different, the core idea of both concepts is that we eventually reach a heavenly state through merit, suffering or a combination of both. In one way or another, <u>we do it.</u> In any guise, this entire concept is contrary to God's Word.

In Romans 4, the Holy Spirit through the Apostle Paul uses the analogy of banking to describe salvation through Jesus Christ. By justice, death stands against our account for every sinful thought, word and action. *For the wages of sin is death, but the free gift of God is eternal life through Jesus Christ our Lord.* Romans 6:23. Two transactions are described in Romans 4. The first is the cancellation of our debt to God for our sin. The second transaction is even more wonderful, because the righteous eternal life of Jesus Christ is deposited in our account. Assume for a moment that you were indebted to a bank for $1 billion. You cannot pay even the interest, let alone the principal of the debt. You're totally bankrupt. The first transaction cancels that debt, but by itself would still leave you with nothing. But now imagine that the same banker voluntarily deposits $1 trillion for you in your account, with no preconditions. It's all yours. This example still understates what Jesus Christ has done for His people, but it does express the basic idea of Romans 4.

The false doctrine of purgatory does present a certain surface truth: that we naturally are in debt to God. He created us and gave us life in the first place. We use His earth (Ps. 24) and breathe His air. We use the oil and minerals that He put on the earth. But the doctrine of purgatory portrays God as a banker who insists that we personally repay our obligations to him through enduring fiery suffering. His grace and mercy is eliminated in this picture. In contrast, the Scriptures say, *Blessed are they to whom the Lord does not impute iniquity, whose sins are covered. Blessed is the man to whom the Lord will not impute sin.* Romans 4:7-8, quoting Psalm 32:1-2.

A second distortion is that we are capable of paying our own sin-debt, according to the doctrine of purgatory. To start repaying the debt, we would have to become perfect and then begin our supposed suffering. If we were not already perfect, we would compound the debt by continuous additional thoughts and words of sin (and of sinful actions and omissions if we were capable of action). Because the wages of all sin is death, we would be multiplying death sentences to ourselves every instant, just as a mass killer like Hitler or Usama bin Laden would multiply deserved judicial death sentences to himself every time his killing regime caused the death of another person. How can we pay even the interest on such a debt? Surely the debt mounts faster than our suffering could possibly pay. Truthfully, we cannot pay for the least of our sin by suffering.

What does purgatory say about the character of God? It teaches that after we have been made perfect and have stopped sinning we still must suffer, perhaps for millions of years. Once perfect, we would then and there be fit for fellowship with God. Why then is suffering still necessary? The doctrine of purgatory paints God as an exacting banker with no shred of mercy to us. In effect, it denies that Jesus Christ through His death paid for the sins of anyone. Is this what the Holy Spirit says through the Bible?

To the contrary, the wonderful promise of God to His people in 2 Corinthians 5 is:

1. While we are present in this body, we are for the present time absent from the Lord;

2. When we are absent from this body, we shall be present with the Lord (and not some place of intermediate suffering!); and

3. Our current bodies will be replaced by new bodies which live eternally. These immortal bodies will be like the everlasting body of Jesus Christ Himself! Consider also 1 Corinthians 15:45-50 and Philippians 3:21.

An example of this promise at work is the repentant thief crucified with Christ Jesus. Surely that thief had no more time to perform good works on earth. He was a guilty violent lawbreaker who admitted that his death sentence was just. Luke 23:41. Then this dying man prayed to Jesus, *Lord, remember me when you come into your kingdom.* Did Jesus warn this man of suffering to come for his past sins? A thousand times no! Our Lord Jesus said instead, *Today you shall be with Me in paradise.* Luke 23:43. **Today** (my emphasis), said our Lord, and not some indefinite future time. This is a specific example of the promise of 2 Corinthians 5 that absence from the body for any believer means the very presence of Jesus Christ.

The false doctrine of purgatory also denies that Jesus Christ has already paid for the sins of His people. To return to the banking example, suppose your father paid your debt to the bank. Could the banker then insist that you pay it again? Of course not, even though the lender might argue that it is unfair that you personally did not bear the cost of repayment. The debt is paid once for all and the debtor is free of the debt. Jesus as High Priest made one sacrifice of Himself to make full and final payment for the sins of His people. Hebrews 7:27. With the debt paid, God will remember our sins no more. Hebrews 8:12. The risen Jesus Christ has already obtained eternal redemption for us and entered once into the Holy Place to present His blood as a permanent atonement for our sins. Hebrews 9:12. We can receive now the promise of inherited eternal life through Jesus Christ. Hebrews 9:15. Hebrews 9:25-28 makes it clear that, Jesus having paid in full for our sins once, no further payment can or will ever be required. In everlasting thankfulness and love let us live for Him now and forever.

Having received this incalculable gift through God's grace and mercy alone by faith alone, we are indeed morally obligated to live for Jesus Christ forever. Good works do come but not until after salvation has been given. Good works play no part in causing salvation. See Romans 9:11, Ephesians 2:9. Public profession of faith and good works are evidence of living faith and salvation. Matthew 10:32, James 2:14-26. James' usage of "justified" is as a matter of evidence, not as a matter of causation. Should there be any doubt, consider Galatians 2:16:

> *Knowing that a man is not justified by the works of the law, but by the faith of Jesus Christ, even we have believed in Jesus Christ, that we might be justified by the faith of Christ, and not by the works of the law: for by the works of the law shall no flesh be justified.*

Consider also Ephesians 2:8-10:

> *For by grace are you saved through faith, and that not of yourselves. It is the gift of*

God, not of works, lest any man should boast. For we are His workmanship, created in Christ Jesus unto good works, which God has before ordained that we should walk in them.

Good works are the result of salvation; salvation is not in any way the result of good works or given in exchange for our suffering or endurance. So let us in everlasting gratitute receive the gift of salvation as a free gift which we have not earned in any way. By the same token, we can live without fear that God will change His mind and take His gift back. As God did with David when David sinned over Uriah and Bathsheba, God disciplined David severely but did not take His gift back. *For the gifts and calling of God are without repentance.* Romans 11:29. Thanks be to God!

APPENDIX B

The "Legislator's Dilemma"

Before directly considering in more detail the differences between Moses' Law and our Lord Jesus' teaching on divorce, we should have a thumbnail of some political truths that are rooted in spiritual truths in the Bible. Many people are under the illusion that there is no relationship between political and spiritual truth. The writers of the Declaration of Independence and of the American Constitution knew better, as did spiritually-minded men such as Winston Churchill and Alexis de Tocqueville, the author of <u>Democracy in America,</u> who said "When America ceases to be good, she will cease to be great."

One truth is the necessity of human government. This appears in Genesis 9 when Noah was commanded by God that murderers should be executed. To consider this further, imagine a society when raiders could enter and pillage your house at any time and even kill, steal and rape without punishment. In fact, some Communist societies such as the Khmer Rouge in Cambodia (The Killing Fields) have come close to this with the elite governing Communist party killing whom they wanted -- about 25% of the population in about 6 years. Virtually every home would have to be an armed castle. Sleep would be almost impossible unless one had a larger group who could keep watch in shifts at night. In fact, Western Europe just after the fall of the Roman Empire was nearly this bad. Feudalism arose when helpless farmers or peasants sold themselves to someone in the neighborhood who had enough military skill to protect them from other raiders. Even serfdom was preferable to anarchy. This era is called the Dark Ages for good reason. Similarly, when the rule of the Biblical judges was breaking down, the elders of the people asked Samuel for a king. 1 Samuel 8:1-7. This was not God's best counsel, but the need for government rather than anarchy or selfish judges was real in the face of nations arising around Israel. It would have been better to have asked Samuel for a better system for God to raise up judges like Gideon (Judges 8:22-23 is tremendous, but note also the failure in Judges 8:24-27), but Israel wanted to be "like the nations."

The next truth, as found in 1 Samuel 8, is that absolute rule by anyone other than by Jesus Christ is a great evil. In the face of Israel's rejection of God in favor of a human king, God tempered His judgment with mercy in granting the nation a king in response to the ill-judged request by keeping political leadership and religious leadership separate. The first king came from Benjamin; the other kings came from Judah. All of the priests came from Levi. But this institutional separation of religious and political leadership does not mean that religious principles are absent from politics. The point is that human leadership of any well-governed nation is divided. An example where this division was of great benefit to Judah is found in 2 Kings 11, where the High Priest safeguarded the last heir of David to the throne and was able to organize a revolt to overthrow and kill the wicked usurper Athaliah.

Samuel's warning of the evils of absolute monarchy in terms of heavy taxation rings through history to the present day. Even Solomon, the wisest of all short of Jesus Christ, succumbed to the temptation of excessive taxation. 1 Kings 12:4. Rehoboam provoked a secession of 10 tribes by warning of still heavier taxation. This secession led to idolatrous worship among the northern tribes and to occasional wars between Israel and Judah. Eventually, the Northern Kingdom was swept away by Assyria and most of the descendents of these tribes are still scattered to remote parts of the earth. Israeli scholars are trying to track down the scattered tribes as I write. Judah (with much of Benjamin, Levi and Simeon within Judah) was conquered by Babylon and exiled also and then scattered again by the Romans after the war of which Jesus warned in Matthew 24, Mark 13 and Luke 21. If Israel had remained united, none of these tragedies would have been likely to occur as in the way that they actually did (although God's judgment cannot be avoided past some point of no return). Joseph in Egypt took 20% of the crop (Genesis 41:34). The total tithes and offerings are said to be roughly the same. The heavy taxes of which Samuel warned on top of the tithes and offerings have indeed caused great misery. American tax rates (combined,

Federal, State and local) are high enough in Biblical terms to be a danger signal in themselves. The French Revolution was triggered by excessive taxation and deficit spending.

The American Constitutional approach to making government strong enough to keep order but restrained enough to respect individual freedom was to divide power among three branches of the Federal government and to divide government power between the central government and the states. The Bill of Rights was an early reinforcement of individual rights from Federal intrusion. Congress was in turn divided into two branches to check each other. *Where no counsel is, the people fall: but in the multitude of counsellors there is safety.* Proverbs 11:14. No system of government is perfect, and even a good system will break down eventually in the sustained grip of wicked rulers. But absolute monarchy turns sour much more quickly. Divided power has a buffering effect that can give time for a wound to heal itself. Consider how drastically English leadership changed from Henry VIII, Edward VI, Queen Mary and Queen Elizabeth I. From the death of Henry VIII to the accession of Elizabeth I was less than 12 years, with dramatic changes in English policy and burnings at the stake under Queen Mary. For an American comparison to show the beneficial buffering effect of divided power, one has George H.W. Bush, Bill Clinton, George W. Bush and Barack Obama. There certainly have been changes, but not with nearly as much whipsaw as with England's monarchy from 1546-1558.

Absolute monarchy hopes that the king or queen will have good sense. An American-type system assumes that rulers will be sinful and seeks to minimize damage and give time to heal the damage that does occur. If the

President and other leaders do have good sense, that's a bonus. There is also a recognition that government will attract people who are tempted by power, with the idea that several powerful men with check the worst in each other. If there is one power-crazed king, that is a quick prescription for misery and terror. *As a roaring lion, and a ranging bear; so is a wicked ruler over the poor people.* Proverbs 28:15. *When the righteous are in authority, the people rejoice: but when the wicked beareth rule, the people mourn.* Proverbs 29:2.

We spoke briefly of the "legislator's dilemma" when discussing the difference between Moses' law of divorce in Deuteronomy 24:1-4 and Christ's teaching as stated in Matthew 19:1-10. The term is my shorthand expression for the problem that any Christian political leader faces when leading a community or nation that is not made up predominantly of the faithful. Our Lord Jesus explained that Moses permitted divorce for "uncleanness" because of the "hardness of your hearts." He was saying that Moses' law permitted conduct below the minimum standard expected of any righteous person. Moses' law was inspired by God as is all Scripture, but it was intended to govern a secular and ungodly community.

Do we face similar dilemmas in modern legislation? Yes. Pro-life Christians frequently have to support laws permitting abortion in cases of rape and incest even though this is wrong in principle. It is not the baby's fault that his or her life originated in a terrible, ungodly act. But such language is the price that today must be paid for enactment of any curbs on abortion at all. With sadness, Christians with experience in this field reason that it is better to stop many infant murders in the womb through compromise rather than to permit infant murders at will by insisting on more perfect legislation that cannot obtain the necessary support. I have personal experience with a variation of this dilemma in supporting candidates whose stance on abortion is imperfect but distinctly better than a candidate whose stance is outright pro-death.

Total prohibition of alcohol is an interesting case to study for those who want to delve deeper into the "legislator's dilemma." Christians early led the Temperance movement because of the havoc caused by drunkenness. It is estimated that in 1835 that Americans drank an average of about 7 gallons of whiskey per year, with predictable horrible results. Gradually more states and localities became "dry." But there were cultures in which consumption of some alcohol was important in addition to the saloons and speakeasies that were places of regular drunkenness and associated evils. During the Prohibition Era, there was indeed a decline in accidents both on and off work, which more modern analysis attributes partially to Prohibition. It should be noted in this case that the Scriptures do require total sobriety but they do not require total abstinence from alcohol. In fact our Lord made wine for the wedding.

I recommend abstinence from alcohol unless medically indispensible without insisting on it as a Biblical requirement because:

A) At least in America, consumption of alcohol is likely to give offense to believers;

B) There are many who are predisposed to becoming alcohol addicts, and I do not wish to be a reason why one such person might stumble into such addiction.

No one can be sure of his or her own predisposition, although if there is a family history of alcohol abuse the probability is high that your system is predisposed also;

C) Most people consume alcohol to "take the edge off of life" or to get "buzzed." This is exactly what the Scriptures forbid in insisting on complete sobriety at least when healthy. God expects us to use 100% of our brainpower to worship and serve Him so long as our bodily condition permits; and

D) Alcohol often contributes to money problems and also has empty calories for little or no benefit except in rare cases (for exceptions see Proverbs 31:6).

To return to the "legislative dilemma," supporters of total Prohibition went beyond the Scriptures in an effort to eliminate several social evils. The effort partially succeeded but also aroused enough antagonism that Prohibition was abandoned after 15 years. This history is an illustration of the problem of how far our legislation can mirror a Christian's life.

In contrast to alcohol, many drugs such as marijuana, cocaine, methamphetamines and heroin cannot be taken without losing sobriety as soon as the drug takes effect. Chinese experience with heroin shows that we must control these drugs strictly in order to maintain cohesion as a nation. In these cases maintenance of Christian standards is vital not only in personal life but also in legislation. In fact the use of mind-altering drugs such as these will be one reason why God will bring the Last Judgment upon the earth. Revelation 9:21 (the word *sorceries* translates the Greek word *pharmakos*).

I'm sure that you will hear that "you can't legislate

morality." You will also hear arguments that Biblical standards are irrelevant to legislation. Nonsense! Should we drop laws against theft and fraud because we are legislating the Eighth Commandment? Should we repeal laws against murder because we are legislating the Sixth Commandment? Should we repeal laws against perjury because they are rooted in the Ninth Commandment against false witness? Of course not! I grant that we cannot enact criminal legislation against covetousness because it represents thought alone rather than action, but the Fifth through Ninth Commandments appear to represent a minimum universal standard for human governments and for human society and civilization. It may be true that we cannot legislate perfect morality or pass laws that will suppress all sin, but it does not follow that there must be no effort to establish morals or to restrain sin even though the efforts and outcomes will be imperfect.

Even before the Law of Moses was given by God to Israel, He had given the command to Noah that murderers were thereafter to be executed, even though Cain was not. Genesis 9:6. Capital punishment under the Law of Moses was expanded to include kidnaping, rape, adultery, cursing a parent (Exodus 21:17; Leviticus 20:9) and blaspheming God (Leviticus 24:15-16), among other offenses. Can we transport the Law of Moses intact from Israel to America? Much as one might prefer to do so, this probably cannot be done because the Law of Moses as it governs political and civil life was never given to a predominantly Gentile nation. Should every nation study its provisions and apply as many of them as practical? Yes!

The "legislator's dilemma" will disappear when the Lord Jesus returns to earth. *"The kingdoms of this world are become the kingdoms of our Lord, and of his Christ; and He shall reign for ever and ever."* Revelation 11:15. All governments of every country shall fall. The checks and balances that are wise and important now in American government shall be swept away because the rulers will no longer be sinful human beings. Instead there will be a single all-wise, all-knowing and all-powerful perfect King (in contrast to every king that has ever ruled a nation before) -- Jesus Christ. No succession plan will be necessary because He will never die or lose His power. No checks and balances will be needed because of His sinless perfection. He will have the power to establish all laws. Because His Father is the ultimate Author of the Law of Moses, I would expect that Jesus will proclaim and enforce an updated version of Moses' Law without the sacrifices and other elements peculiar to Israel's existence before Jesus was first born in human flesh. Crimes that were capital under Moses' law will again be capital under Jesus Christ. By studying Moses' law, we can have a good outline of what such a law code would be like. (See Isaiah 2:2-3, where it is prophesied that *the Law will go forth from Zion...*) It will be superior to all that has come before, especially because the perfect and incorruptible Judge will enforce it. At long last Satan -- the lawless one -- will be put down forever and the very need for law will disappear because sin itself will be confined to the Lake of Fire. Hallelujah!

Appendix C

A Thumbnail On Holiness In General

Does genuine conversion to Christianity make a difference in one's character and conduct? You bet! Ephesians 2 through 5 is especially strong on this theme. But for some it may be easier to see the impact of conversion on either (1) one person's life before and after his or her conversion; or (2) differences between two prominent people who lived in similar times and cultures. I will ask you to read the letter to the Ephesians for yourself and to consider the contrast between the lives of the children of disobedience (2:2) and wrath (2:3) on the one hand and people who are the workmanship of God (2:10) on the other.

PETER V. JUDAS

Peter and Judas were obviously contemporaries and both apparent disciples of our Lord Jesus Christ. They traveled the same roads, heard the same sermons, saw the same miracles and saw the same changes in people caused by the Master's touch. So immediate environmental influences do not explain their obviously different finishes to their lives.

Both showed sin. Judas was a thief (John 12:6), specifically an embezzler because he took from the common purse. When our Lord Jesus received worship in the form of anointing with expensive oil, Judas was especially disappointed that oil was not sold and given to the poor. The sale proceeds would have been put into the common purse first, and Judas would have had an opportunity to skim his cut before the gift would have been made. In spirit, Judas was similar to Ananias and Sapphira in Acts 5. But Peter was also sinful. While he did received revelation from the Father that Jesus was the promised Messiah (Matthew 16:17-18), Peter resisted Jesus' plan to die on the Cross. (Matthew 16:21-23) Peter even tried to put up armed resistance to the arresting soldiers in the Garden of Gethsemane. (John 18:10-11) Peter's resistance to our Lord's word that He would give His life as a ransom for many (Matthew 20:28) extended for a substantial period of time -- it was not an isolated misunderstanding. Then Peter boasted of his willingness to die for his Master (John 13:36-38) but proved a coward after his armed resistance was stopped by Jesus Himself. (John 18:15-17; 25-27) Before we become judgmental over Peter's faults, we should remember these points:

A) Peter did not yet have the Holy Spirit within. That was to come in Acts 2 at Pentecost, almost 2 months later. This newfound power of the Spirit made a radical difference in Peter's life;

B) It was not yet Peter's time to die. God permit Peter's natural cowardice to show through because He was preserving Peter for church leadership. This had the dual effect of making Peter understand his own weakness in order to fit him for ministry and of keeping Roman scrutiny on the Lamb of God and away from the apostles who were to be the first leaders of the church. Even when Peter was spiritually stronger and ready enough to die that he would be sound asleep on the night before his scheduled execution, God intervened through an angel a second time to free Peter from prison because it still was not Peter's time to die. Acts 12.

C) There was tremendous spiritual pressure such as seldom been seen at the time of the Crucifixion. (Luke 22:53) Even Jesus Himself felt it. (John 13:21) Satan entered into Judas when he took the sop from Jesus. (John 13:26-27) Jesus sweated blood praying in the Garden. (Luke 22:44) The guards fell down when they first approached Jesus. (John 18:6) While we can and should learn from Peter's failures to distrust our own flesh, we should not imagine that we are strong enough spiritually to have done better unless we had special strengthening from the Spirit for such pressure. (Compare Mark 13:11 and Luke 21:14 forbidding us to imagine what we might say if arrested for Jesus' sake, because if we must face such pressure we will be told at that time -- not before -- what to say).

What made the difference between Peter and Judas? Jesus prayed for Peter (Luke 22:31-34). There is no indication that Jesus prayed for Judas (note that "the world" is excluded from Jesus' prayer in John 17:9). In fact, Jesus knew from the beginning of His training of the disciples that Judas would betray Him (John 6:64) and even made reference to the offense that would come. (Luke 17:1) Ultimately, it is Jesus' intercession for us in His resurrected life that is our life preserver that keeps us for heaven and holiness. This is likewise true of the Holy Spirit.

> *Likewise the Spirit also helps our infirmities: for we know not what we should pray for as we ought: but the Spirit itself makes intercession for us with groanings which cannot be uttered. And he that searches the hearts knows what is the mind of the Spirit, because he maketh intercession for the saints according to the will of God. Romans 8:26-7.*

> *Who is he that condemns? It is Christ that died, yea rather, that is risen again, who is even at the right hand of God, Who also makes intercession for us. Romans 8:34.*

So what differences did the intercession of Christ Jesus for Peter make between Peter and Judas? Judas took a bribe to betray Jesus, went through seller's remorse and threw the money back and then committed suicide even before Jesus was crucified (Matthew 27:3-5). Peter was restored by our Lord Jesus (John 21). Peter became bold and courageous, as shown by his sermon in Acts 2 less than 2 months after the authorities crucified the Lord Jesus. He called upon his listeners to repent of their sins (including those who had their part in the Crucifixion, most or all of whom were still in Jerusalem at this early date) and be baptized. This boldness reminds one of

John the Baptist, who was beheaded a short time earlier for rebuking one of the rulers for his sexual immorality in marrying his brother's divorced wife. Peter became first among the apostles and led the Jerusalem church in its early days. As one reads through Acts 1-12, we find Peter involved with healings, more preaching to Jews and the initial opening of the Gospel to the Gentiles and the judgment of Ananias and Sapphira and of the sorcerer who sought to buy the Holy Spirit. Peter even raised one woman from the dead through the power granted to him. Peter defended Paul against accusations that he was going too far in reaching out to the Gentiles. Peter wrote two epistles, and most scholars believe that Peter influenced strongly the Gospel of Mark. Even though Peter was inconsistent in temporarily withdrawing from Gentile Christians (Galatians 2:11-13), Peter led a remarkably productive life. So the intercession of Jesus Christ was answered abundantly and Peter became a holy and loyal man of God in contrast to the traitor Judas.

THE APOSTLE PAUL

If Peter is the most prominent figure in the first portion of Acts, then Paul is the most prominent in the second portion. Paul (then named Saul, for the king of Israel who had been from Saul's tribe of Benjamin -- to distinguish him from other men named Saul, he was often called Saul of Tarsus, the city of his childhood) first appears at the lynching of Stephen in Acts 7 (using stones instead of a noose, but a lawless mob death nonetheless), not as having thrown a stone himself, but as having held the coats of those who did. Acts 7:58, 8:1. Saul was then the driving force behind a persecution of Christians that extended beyond Jerusalem and Judea to Damascus. The reason why the Damascus Christians were going to be dragged back to Jerusalem was to try them before the Sanhedrin -- the same court that had condemned Jesus Christ to death. Then the Sanhedrin would pressure the Romans for mass crucifixions backed by the threat of Jewish non-cooperation or even uprising if Christians were tolerated. This plan was destroyed by Jesus Himself appearing to Paul on the Damascus Road and converting Paul. But we should not imagine that Jesus was reacting to a human plan that He had not foreseen before it was hatched. In fact, the conversion of Paul was planned from Paul's conception in his mother's womb (Galatians 1:15). The ministry and suffering of Paul was planned beforehand (Acts 9:15-16) and gradually unfolded to Paul.

What can we observe about Paul's character before his salvation on the Damascus Road? He was zealous, which can be a good thing if directed rightly. He was also an angry young man with virtually no sense of restraint. Paul was ruthless. After his conversion Paul remained zealous and hard-working, but patience and gentleness were introduced into his character which were foreign to his previous nature. 1 Thessalonians 2:11; 2 Corinthians 6:4, 12:12. The Corinthian church was especially trying because it had many gifts but also many troubles. Once convinced of the truth of the resurrection of Jesus Christ, Paul did not waver thereafter. The miracles that Paul performed through the Holy Spirit is similar in nature to those of Peter, although there were more of them in Paul's life. (1 Corinthians 15:10; 2 Corinthians 11:23-28) If one takes a close comparison in Acts, it appears that there is a corresponding miracle in Paul's life to each of the miracles of Peter, with the possible exception of the deaths of Ananias and Sapphira. The holiness that Jesus Christ introduced into Paul's life changed a man who had the potential to become an ancient Hitler to the single greatest champion of the Christian faith after Christ Himself.

KING SAUL V. KING DAVID
(for detail, read 1 and 2 Samuel and selected Psalms)

These were successive kings of Israel. We estimate Saul's reign from 1040 B.C. to about 1000 B.C. David's reign is specified to have been 40 years. We estimate his death at 960 B.C. The first seven years were in Hebron fighting a civil war against the forces of Saul's surviving son Ishbosheth. Abner was the mainspring of the forces of the tribe of Benjamin, and Shimei tried to revive Benjamite rule during Absolom's uprising. The last thirty-three years of David's rule were in the new capital of Jerusalem which David captured from the descendents of the Jebusites who had fooled Joshua into an alliance contrary to God's original command. Its importance has been revived today and is the flash-point of contention between Jew and Muslim. *Pray for the peace of Jerusalem.* Psalm 122:6.

This condensed historical survey is one hint of the character differences between Saul and David. While Saul had continued Samson's work of liberating Israel from raids and subjugation by its surrounding enemies (especially the Philistines), at the end of Saul's life that progress was in ruins and Saul himself was a suicide when his army was crushed by the Philistines on Mount Gilboa.

Three of his children, including the magnificent Jonathan (who at God's Word was willing to take second place to David even though he was the son of the king -- God allowed him honorable death in battle because David would never have had an undisturbed reign while Jonathan was alive. Ishbosheth was a much weaker character, and yet Benjamin still maintained a civil war on his behalf) were also killed during the same disastrous battle. Saul left very little as a lasting legacy.

David's influence is still felt today. He made Jerusalem the capital of Israel and brought the Ark of the Covenant there to the place where Abraham had been prepared to sacrifice Isaac and received God's provision of a lamb in place of his son. David did the design work for the first Temple and gathered the materials for its construction before his death. He also settled Solomon as his successor, founding a royal dynasty that lasted nearly 400 years after his death and continued without the throne thereafter. Most important of all, David received a covenant from God that one of his descendents would be the promised Messiah, the ultimate King of Israel and the Son of David Who would be the Savior of people of all races. (2 Samuel 7 -- compare Matthew 20:30-31; 22:42-46 and the geneologies given by Matthew and Luke, both of which take care to point out that Jesus Christ was a lineal descendent of David). If I were a university professor of Biblical history, I believe that it would be justified academically to spend an entire 3-hour semester course on David alone. The Lord Jesus, His ultimate successor as King of Israel (John 1:49) would occupy several such courses and we would still be far from truly fathoming Him.

Getting back to the differences in character between Saul and David, two little-studied incidents stand out as bellweathers. Saul foolishly insisted that Israel fight the Philistines on empty stomachs. 1 Samuel 14. (Napoleon knew better; he said that an army marches on its stomach. Food for its fighting men has been a strong point in American military history ever since the bitter experience of Morristown.) Jonathan, having not been present when the order was given, ate honey and violated his father's order that he did not receive. Saul wanted to kill Jonathan even though Jonathan had been God's instrument of victory that day. The people restrained Saul. David faced a situation where 200 of his 600 men were so exhausted that they could not continue the pursuit of the Midianites who had raided David's camp at Ziklag. David left them to guard the baggage train and continued with the other 400 to recapture the men's families and to take other spoils from the raiders. David issued a permanent command that the men guarding the baggage share equally with the men able to go forward. 1 Samuel 30. Where Saul was arbitrary and denied his soldiers needed nourishment, David took care of his fighting men (with the terrible and sinful exception of Uriah and Bathsheba).

Even with the terrible blot of David's murder of Uriah in order to cover his sin of adultery with Bathsheba (2 Samuel 11-12), the general course of David's spiritual life was upward, though with periodic troughs from David's tangled family life stemming from his polygamy and his adultery/murder. David triumphed over Goliath at the start of his career and triumphed over Satan at the end of his life. The course of Saul's life was downward spiritually.

Saul started well against Nahash (1 Samuel 11) but soon disobeyed God in offering sacrifice without Samuel as the priest (1 Samuel 13) and then in sparing Agag's life when God had commanded his execution (1 Samuel 15). Saul was jealous of David because of David's initial success in killing Goliath and then his popularity with the people of Israel. 1 Samuel 18:7-8. Saul hurled a spear at David and missed (1 Samuel 18:9-10). This developed into an immense manhunt with the intent of killing David. In the course of this Saul's agent Doeg slaughtered the priests (1 Samuel 22). David spared Saul's life twice because Saul had been God's anointed. David was willing to wait for God to kill Saul in His time so that David would be the legitimate king without shedding blood in the process. Saul grew so worried that he even consulted a witch -- strictly forbidden by Moses' law, as Saul well knew -- the night before his death (1 Samuel 28:5-25). Then Saul killed himself near the end of the lost battle.

David's spiritual course was upward on the whole even with two great failures: the sins of adultery and murder involving Uriah and Bathsheba and the numbering of the people (2 Samuel 24). Even though David lost four children by reason of his sin involving Uriah and Bathsheba, he was forgiven (Psalms 38, 51 and 32) and actually finished his earthly life a joyous and triumphant man. (Psalm 18; 2 Samuel 22 -- consider also Psalms 16 and 24). We know the depth of the grace and forgiveness of God in considerable part through David. David has given us much concerning the Lord Jesus (for example, Psalms 2, 22, 23, 45 and 110 plus portions of many others). David wrote approximately half of the Psalms, which are a portion of the enduring Word of God. David will live forever with his Lord, Savior and descendent Jesus Christ.

QUEEN MARY V. QUEEN ELIZABETH I

We are now looking at later historical rather than Biblical examples. Queen Mary, sometimes known as "Bloody Mary," reigned in England from 1553 into 1558. Her husband was Philip II King of Spain, who later sent the Spanish Armada against England. Queen Elizabeth I was Queen Mary's successor, who reigned from 1558 into 1604. For historical context, Martin Luther had died nearly the same time as Henry VIII of England (the father of both Queen Mary and Queen Elizabeth) and John Calvin and John Knox (Reformers in Geneva and in Scotland who have strongly influenced Christian theology even into modern times) were alive during Queen Mary's reign and during the early part of the reign of Queen Elizabeth. While Queen Mary was thought to be secure through the alliance with Spain, she died relatively young. While Queen Elizabeth I was thought to be a likely candidate for early death because she had no foreign alliance of any consequence and incurred Spanish anger for support of Dutch freedom of conscience, she lived an essentially normal life span and died without violence. Neither had children; Queen Elizabeth I never married. There were numerous plots to assassinate Queen Elizabeth, but all of them were foiled. Many were stopped by Walsingham and his agents, who were forerunners of England's famed MI-5 and of the American FBI and CIA.

The differences between Queen Mary and Queen Elizabeth I were stark. In religion and politics, Queen Mary stood for absolute monarchy, Papal supremacy and for execution of any whose conscience disagreed. It is estimated that approximately 500 people in England and Wales (Scotland was still independent then) were burned to death at the stake for holding to the Biblical faith during Queen Mary's reign. Two of them had been bishops in the Church of England during the brief but important reign of Edward VI between the reign of Henry VIII and Queen Mary. Others were common people who had read their Scriptures. This averages to about two per week. Given the much smaller area and lower population, this was truly a substantial number of executions for religious causes.

When Queen Mary died, there were more executions scheduled. The death of the Queen required that the death warrants be signed anew by the incoming Queen Elizabeth. Instead, she ordered the prisoners freed and the executions stopped. Queen Elizabeth reversed most of Queen Mary's basic policies. She believed in England's independence from all foreign powers and adjusted her diplomacy accordingly. England became a quiet enemy of the Counter-Reformation because her people and her Queen stood for the supremacy of the Crown over the Pope in church matters and liberty of religious conscience in general principle. (In truth, Jesus Christ is Head of the Church, and not Pope, Monarch, nor Church Council. For example, see Mark 12:11; Ephesians 5:23; Colossians 1:18. The idea of the King or Queen as Head of the Church did cause trouble in later generations.) Most importantly, the Bible became freely available to anyone in England in the language of the people. In Elizabeth's day, this usually meant the Geneva Bible which the Pilgrims brought to America. About 7 years after Queen Elizabeth's death, the King James translation, underwritten by the Crown, was finished in 1611. While Queen Elizabeth I did not allow full religious freedom in the modern American sense of the term, she did allow the Scriptures to be taught regularly and Biblical teaching flourished. So did literature; Shakespeare is one well-known example. When Elizabeth was Princess under his older sister's reign, she gave minimal conformity to the Papal forms enforced by Queen Mary, but abandoned them upon her death for Anglican worship composed by Thomas Cranmer, a Reformer and martyr under Queen Mary. In all likelihood Queen Elizabeth herself trusted in Jesus Christ, although only He can be the judge of that.

To understand our own American roots, we need a basic knowledge of the history of England in Queen Elizabeth's time. When Dutch patriots rose against Philip II's Spanish forces, Elizabeth gave some discreet assistance and later a few troops. While taxes were one major cause of the Dutch revolt, freedom of religious conscience was another critical element. This was a family quarrel of sorts; Philip II was Elizabeth's brother-in-law when he was married to Queen Mary before her death. He showed some interest in marrying Elizabeth too, but she declined. Events in Scotland led to the overthrow of Mary, Queen of Scots (actually French in her basic outlook, and not to be confused with the deceased Mary who was Elizabeth's half-sister and predecessor). The Queen of Scots was also next in line for the English throne. She sought refuge in Elizabeth's realm. Elizabeth granted it but imprisoned her in a comfortable castle. The deposed Queen of Scots was nominally Papal in her religion but in essence was a headstrong woman without self-control or discretion. There is little doubt that Mary, Queen of Scots would have destroyed such religious freedom as did exist under Elizabeth had she obtained the power to do so. Many English people thought the Queen of Scots dangerous because of her incentive to cause Elizabeth's death if she could get away with it. At length Walsingham's agents uncovered proof of plotting by Mary, Queen of Scots, to assassinate Queen Elizabeth to take the throne for herself. Reluctantly, Queen Elizabeth ordered the execution of Mary, Queen of Scots, not because of religion but because of the murder plots. This in turn provoked Philip II of Spain to change from a "cold war" with Elizabethan England to all-out attack with the Spanish Armada to combine with Spain's army in the Netherlands; he was genuinely shocked that a royal queen, even deposed, could be subject to law and especially to the death penalty. To execute royalty under penalty of law was admittedly novel at that time. He also realized that there was no further hope of reconciliation between Spain and England except by conquest. Success in the attack would mean that Philip would effectively rule England and that Papal legates would unleash a new round of executions for maintaining the faith of the Scriptures.

Thus, in 1588 the Spanish Armada, thought to be the strongest fleet in the world, sailed from Spain to England. The result is well-known; what the English Navy but started, God completed with a storm wind that blew the Armada through the North Sea north of Scotland. The Spanish Navy never recovered fully from this defeat. This meant that the Spanish Navy was unable to prevent

English and French colonization of North America. The French colony in Quebec would be nourished and new English colonies would eventually expand and become the United States of America. Spain gradually declined while France and England rose in strength. The Netherlands at length secured full independence from Spain. In the 20th century, the Netherlands contributed Corrie ten Boom (The Hiding Place) and Brother Andrew (God's Smuggler) among others to the Body of Christ. Indirectly, all this and more pivoted on the accession and character of Queen Elizabeth I, whom God placed on the throne of England and maintained in power for about 45 years. Yes, Christian holiness (and statecraft in this case through the providence of God) can be that important! Another case in English history which shows the importance of one person is the nanny who taught Christianity to Winston Churchill.

John Wesley, George Whitfield & Methodism

Methodism in the 18th and 19th centuries was a mighty revival movement which called people throughout the English-speaking world to salvation and holiness. They were called Methodists because they sought to live godly lives through maintaining habits of Biblical conduct. They were methodical in their approach -- hence the name Methodists. John Wesley and George Whitfield were its most famous preachers in the 18th century; they preached on both sides of the Atlantic. There were countless circuit riding preachers who rode on horseback far into the countryside to give country folk some measure of Biblical preaching from a trained, educated preacher. Some of these men are scarcely known to history, but

they are known to God. I will give one example of the
impact of the preaching of John Wesley. He went to a
certain town, provoking one of the leading men in the
community to complain to the magistrate about Wesley's
presence and preaching. The complainer and his friends
had noticed a change in their wives. They had gone from
sharp-tongued to being as meek as lambs. When the man
complained to the magistrate, the magistrate was wiser.
His reaction was that he would desire that Wesley would
convert all of the common scolds in the town.

This is not to say that women should never speak up.
There are times when a woman's speech can do great
good. Deborah (Judges 4-5) and Huldah (2 Kings 22; 2
Chronicles 34) were prophetesses. Anna just after our
Lord's birth prophesied of His future redeeming work
(Luke 2:36-38). The ideal woman of Proverbs 31:26 has
the law of kindness in her speech. The magistrate may
have known 1 Peter 3:4, which says that a meek and quiet
spirit of great value for any woman. The main point here
is that godly preaching by men such as Wesley and
Whitfield impacted the hearts, minds, speech and actions
of their hearers and in this instance changed the wives
first.

One should wonder why the men complained when
their home life should have been more pleasant when
their wives changed their way of speaking. I do not know,
but I can make some reasonable guesses. One is that the
men used their wives' sharp tongues as excuses for their
own sins. Some might have been yelling at their wives or
even hitting them. Others might have staying out with
the boys and getting drunk and gambling away the family
money or consorting with immoral women. This was

endemic in English society when God raised up Wesley and Whitfield. Whatever the case, the men lost their excuses when their wives became more loving. The obvious change in their wives challenged the men to follow suit. Perhaps these two did not want even wholesome change in their own lives.

I do not know whether or not the complainers were ever brought to Jesus Christ for salvation or not. Even the magistrate had not yet professed salvation in his own life, although he did observe that it was good for the "common scolds." But what about you? Have you had a friend or relative (or even your own spouse) change drastically and try to talk to you about the joy of Jesus Christ? If so, what is your response? Do you brush the person off as one would a housefly or find some less rude way to change the subject? Are you willing to at least inquire with an open mind how your friend has been changed? Are you willing to look at a Bible and read for yourself? Better still, are you willing to ask the Lord Jesus to change you too?

One other Christian revival in Wales starting in 1905 had even broader consequences. There were virtually no court cases for months because crime nosedived and people no longer sought divorces. The coal miners had to retrain the mules in the mines because they stopped cursing. The animals had no understanding of the meaning of the words, but they no longer understood the miners' commands because their speech was gentler and lacked curses. The change was long-lasting. In all likelihood, the father portrayed in *How Green Is My Valley* was a Christian converted as a younger man during this revival.

Brother Andrew

Brother Andrew was a young teenager during the Nazi occupation of his native Netherlands between 1940 and 1945. He was something of a daredevil. When he joined the Dutch Army after World War 2, he volunteered to drive a tank even though he had not driven before. He was able to get the tank started but could not stop properly. God would use this daring later for good after he was converted. Following his salvation and Bible training in England, Brother Andrew was invited by Communists on youth tours of Eastern Europe. As in so many instances, God used these tours for His own purposes by focusing Brother Andrew's attention on Eastern Europe, then under Communist rule. Possession of a Bible was considered a crime. But Brother Andrew risked imprisonment in a concentration camp or even death to bring Bibles to Eastern Europe year after year. Brother Andrew once enjoyed adventure for its own sake, but this daring was harnessed to risk everything for the sake of spreading God's Word. *"The wicked flee when no man pursues: but the righteous are bold as a lion."* Proverbs 28:1.

Charles Colson

Charles Colson first came to prominence as a member of the White House staff under President Nixon during his first term. He said that he would "run over his grand-mother" for President Nixon as an expression of his loyalty. But Colson was involved in criminal activity which led to imprisonment and the loss of his law license. His prison term was cut short because his son had been arrested for possession of marijuana. Now what?

Salvation by faith through the grace of God was the start. God's fuller answer was that Chuck Colson would lead Prison Fellowship, a Christian mission to jails and prisons in America and eventually abroad as well. Charles Colson learned compassion in place of the hard-boiled willingness to "run over his grand-mother." Even if this was a figure of speech and not meant literally, the attitude expressed is far from "*Love your neighbor as yourself*" or "*Love your enemies.*" We have some measure of the impact of the Gospel of Christ on Charles Colson's character and actions by the distance between his political life before Christ and his later life serving prisoners and their families.

To a certain extent Charles Colson's conversion mirrors that of the Apostle Paul almost 20 centuries later. In both cases hard-driving, ruthless men were transformed by the power of God into leaders of love.

These are but sketches of the lives mentioned. These sketches only hint at the spiritual power of Christian holiness. As holiness is necessary as evidence that a claim of salvation is valid, (see Matthew 7:21: "*Not every one that says unto Me, Lord, Lord, shall enter into the kingdom of heaven; but he that does the will of My Father which is in heaven.*") it is also necessary for joy and power in any Christian's life, including yours and mine.

Appendix D

The Character Of God And His Mercy And Judgment

Many would question my description of the disaster awaiting the unfaithful based on arguments from the character of God as a God of love. Indeed He is a God of love, but that is only part of the truth. Admittedly, no finite human being can completely portray the character of God. Stephen Charnock, an old Puritan writer who started to write a systematic theology, started with the character of God and spent the remainder of his life studying that topic alone. Neither he nor anyone else did a complete and accurate description. So long as this is acknowledged, there is acknowledged unavoidable imperfection involved but no deliberate deception. If a portion of the truth is presented as the whole truth, then the presentation becomes a lie made up of pieces of truth taken out of context. There is a strong modern tendency to present the love of God as if it were the entire character of God. But the Scriptures make it clear that the love of God for at least some of the children of Adam is only part of the picture. Romans 9-11 presents a broader view of God Who has chosen to love <u>a portion</u> of fallen humanity and to give the rest what they deserve before His justice. The Apostle Paul points out that God told Moses that *Jacob have I loved but Esau have I hated.* (Romans 9:13) Modern humanity tends to agree with the woman who wants asked C.H. Spurgeon (one of the greatest preachers of London in the 19th century) how God could hate Esau. Spurgeon responded that this was easy to understand when one remembers Esau's life. He traded his birthright for one meal and married three women. Two of them at least were griefs to his parents. For Spurgeon, the difficult thing was how God could love Jacob, the deceiver and supplanter. Romans 9 also contains the example of the division between Ishmael the firstborn and Isaac the child of promise. Further, God raised up Pharaoh (that is, the Pharaoh of the Exodus) to the heights of power for the express purpose of smashing him as a warning to tyrants thereafter and as a warning to the enemies of Israel for the rest of time. Paul told Timothy that God has the right to create vessels of either honor or dishonor and for either beauty or common functionality. 2 Timothy 2:20.

There are several instances in the Bible when God directed that certain families or certain peoples be wiped out because their wickedness. Sodom and Gomorrah were one case where God did not leave the destruction to human responsibility but used angels instead. Certain rebels in Israel were killed by the direct hand of God with no further opportunity to repent. Numbers 16 records the deaths of 250 people and their relatives who transgressed in the worship of God. God burned the 250 from heaven and buried others alive. Other rebels within Israel were bitten fatally by poisonous snakes. Numbers 21:6. The entire generation who feared to enter the Promised Land -- Joshua and Caleb excepted -- were denied entry after they failed to go up by faith. Hebrews 3:9-19. It is true that this generation died only gradually rather than suddenly, but they nevertheless failed to enter the Promised Land because of unbelief.

There are many other cases of God's judgment in the Old Testament. God ordered the destruction of the Canaanites, both because of their wickedness and because they occupied the land that God was giving to Israel. (Deuteronomy 20:16-17) Samuel executed Agag when Saul disobeyed God by sparing him. 1 Samuel 15:32-33 I could point to the destruction of the houses of Jeroboam (1 Kings 15:29) and of Ahab (2 Kings 9). Consider also the Babylonian Captivity recorded in Jeremiah, Ezekiel and Daniel and commented upon at the end of 2 Chronicles. Other examples come from the ministry of our Lord Jesus Christ, Who was the exact image of His Father. (Colossians 1:15). We have many instances of His compassion, but also we have cases where He acted in judgment even though His life in human flesh was not the time for Him to judge the world. We cannot take a rounded view of Jesus' life and conclude that love is His only outstanding attribute.

Our Lord Jesus twice fed an entire mass audience from almost no food. He healed countless people in every conceivable circumstance, from a demon-possessed man living in a cemetery to sick children and a soldier's servant. He showed compassion to a woman taken in adultery (John 8) and to another woman (John 4) of ill repute. He patiently taught Nicodemus (John 3). He forgave sins. Matthew 9:2-6; Luke 7:47-8. He gave His life a ransom for many. Matthew 20:28. Yet he also told leaders of Israel that they would die in their sins, meaning that they would be among the damned because of their unbelief. John 8:21,24. In Matthew 25:46 He spoke of everlasting punishment. In Luke 16:19-31 Jesus told the story of the poor man who died in faith and the rich man who died in his earthly riches but who ignored the poor around him. The rich man found his tongue on fire with no water to quench it. Our Lord Jesus indeed loves sinners as no man has ever loved, but He has an equal passion for justice and righteousness. He defended His Father's honor. (John 5:19ff.) The hypocrite who was forgiven a huge debt but then refused to forgive or even delay a small debt was delivered to the tormentors, implying that those unwilling to forgive will be tormented in the Lake of Fire. Matthew 18:21-30. You can undoubtedly add to both lists by studying the four Gospels, but the basic point is that one needs to consider Jesus Christ as a Man of both mercy and justice. His holiness unites the two. He has the perfect judgment of when to show patience or divine mercy and when to execute judgment. He also has the sovereign right to act as He pleases; our Lord Jesus is not a wimp but He is the Judge of all humanity. From His judgments there is never an appeal.

One of the most moving moments of the Last Judgment will be the confessions of the wicked that Jesus

Christ is Lord. Philippians 2:9-11. Just imagine a scene in which Caiphas and Annas (who tried Jesus at his Sanhedrin trial), Herod the Great (who tried to kill Jesus as an infant), Pilate, Hitler, Lenin, Stalin, Mussolini, Tojo, Mao, Castro, Ho Chi Minh, Ne Win and Pol Pot among many others admit that Jesus Christ is Lord of All. Their confessions will be too late to do them any good and will be extracted from them unwillingly, but they will be real and bring glory to all three Persons of the Godhead. I thank God that through His mercy I will witness this with joy.

The most critical point is that we cannot worship a Jesus of our own devising or imagination, nor can we pick and choose the portions of His character and words that we like. While we will never in this body have a complete and full understanding of Him, we must be willing to worship Him as He is and not as we would prefer Him to be. He demands the same quality of worship that Thomas gave after His resurrection: *My Lord and my God!* John 20:28.

Appendix E

The Judgment Of God From The Standpoint Of Justice

If you accept the general thrust of Biblical teaching about the Lake of Fire, you still may wonder why such awful everlasting punishment is necessary. If you are still inclined to accuse God (or even accuse the Biblical writers of misrepresenting God) of being unduly harsh in teaching everlasting punishment of the wicked dead, I would urge you to ponder the reasons why this doctrine is an integral part of the Christian faith.

To start, let us imagine a terrible villain who has not expressed the least regret for his actions. Some historical examples are Hitler, Stalin, Pol Pot, Mao and Genghis Khan. We might also remember serial murderers such as Jack the Ripper and Jeffrey Dahmer. If someone like one of these people killed a relative of yours, would the fact that the person is now dead satisfy your desire for justice?

If you are like most relatives of decedents who now give victims' statements under current practice before sentence is passed, you probably would not be satisfied with the earthly death of the offender. We sometimes hear language saying something to the effect that "death is too good for this criminal." Our sense of justice calls for something more than simple physical death. Admittedly, our sense of justice is not the final arbiter of right and wrong, but it is part of the conscience that often points us in the right direction.

Did Hitler escape punishment by his suicide? If there is no eternal punishment in the Lake of Fire, we would be compelled to answer yes. We cannot say that death is itself the punishment, because death has come upon all human beings -- even Jesus Christ Himself Who knew no sin (Romans 5:12, 2 Corinthians 5:21). So then have Hitler and other evil men escaped punishment because they were able to evade the law? The Christian answer is that Hitler and similar men who have escaped earthly punishment instead accelerated their divine punishment by their suicide. Even eliminating the suicide element, a criminal who dies without repentance has not "gotten away with it." Genghis Khan said himself that he enjoyed inflicting misery on other men and women by raping the women in the presence of their captive husbands. He died a natural death -- where is his punishment? Or did he really get away with his crimes?

The Apostle Paul through the Holy Spirit gives us an indirect answer to this question in his discussion of the resurrection of the dead. In 1 Corinthians 15:19, Paul said that *"if in this life only we have hope in Christ, we are of all men most miserable."* I would argue that the opposite proposition is also an integral part of the Christian faith and of any belief in divine justice at all. If there is no everlasting punishment for wickedness, then why restrain ourselves from wickedness on earth? Paul quotes Horace, a Latin poet, as saying that *"Let us eat and drink for tomorrow we shall die."* 1 Corinthians 15:32. Paul's immediate context was a false supposition that there is no resurrection. That quotation works logically just as well as a cover for extreme wickedness as it does as a supposed disappointment of the hopes of the righteous.

The honor and truth of God is at stake on this issue. God has commanded his saints not to take revenge themselves because *"Vengeance is Mine. I will repay, says the Lord."* Romans 12:19; Hebrews 10:30. See also Isaiah 35:4, 61:2, 63:4; Deuteronomy 32:35-43; Psalm 58:10, 94:1; Luke 18:7-8. 2 Thessalonians 1:4-10. (There are many more passages on God's vengeance, but I have left out those that might have reference to vengeance on earth to bend over backward to be fair to an opposing view. I have therefore understated the case.) If there is no punishment after death, God's promises to His own people are hollow. In addition, our Lord Jesus Christ, Who warned of "hellfire" during the Sermon on the Mount and taught punishment after death in Luke 16:19-31 as well as in Luke 18:7-8, would be made a liar if there is no punishment after death for the unrighteous. In fact He is the Truth personnified. John 14:6.

God has given us the ability to use logic and reasoning for our use. But these facilities must always be subordinate to the Scriptures themselves. We may expect to find passages of Scripture teaching punishment after death as a necessary corollary of a belief in divine justice, but we must actually search the Scriptures to see if they are really present as we might expect.

Isaiah 14:4 starts a condemnation of the King of Babylon -- most likely Belshazzar, because we know that Nebuchadnezzar (Daniel 4) repented and worshipped God at the end of his long reign. In the context of punishment after death, consider especially verses 9-10:

> *Hell from beneath is moved for you to meet*
> *you at your coming: it stirs up the dead for*
> *you, even all the chief ones of the earth; it*
> *has raised up from their thrones all the kings*
> *of the nations. All they shall speak and say*
> *unto you, Are you also become weak as we?*
> *are you become like unto us?*

From this passage it is clear that the predecessors of the King of Babylon as powerful leaders were aware of his former strength and progress, even though they were dead physically. They were conscious and knew their own weakness and saw the downfall of the King of Babylon. Job asked the question, *"If a man die, shall he live again?"* Job 14:14. His answer there and in Job 19:23-27 is an emphatic Yes! As further evidence, consider that Abraham in Luke 16:19-31 was aware of Moses and of the prophets who had not lived during Abraham's earthly life. For mercy or for punishment, the physically dead do not lose consciousness after physical death.

Is God being unfair or cruel to His own creation? No! It is indeed true that the worst that one human being has done to another pales in comparison to what happens to confirmed rebels in the Lake of Fire. It is unspeakable for one sinful human being to do such things to another, but we have to remember that justice is different when a perfect God is dealing with rebellious humanity. I speak as much of the truth that I can see because I want to warn others to repent, worship Jesus Christ and stay far away from the Lake of Fire. I am like the watchman or sentry (Ezekiel 3, repeated in Ezekiel 33) who has a duty to give as accurate a warning as his knowledge permits, even if the news is grim. Jesus Himself gave His human body to cruel executioners to keep others away from the Lake of Fire. He Himself warned, *"Fear not them which kill the body, but are not able to kill the soul: but rather fear Him which is able to destroy both soul and body in hell."* Matthew 10:28. Our Lord Jesus understand the pain of hell and of the Lake of Fire as nobody else. As to accusing God of being cruel as most of us (including me) would be prone to do, *"No but O man, who are you that replies against God?"* Romans 9:20. Job sought a hearing with God and ended up in abject but blessed repentance. I can only admit that God is right and that the initial inclination of my heart and mind is utterly wrong. One of the blessings that comes from the everlasting punishment of the wicked is the everlasting peace of the righteous. With justice triumphant over Satan and his rebels among both humans and fallen angels, mercy and peace reign triumphant and finally undisturbed among the purified. There can be no undisturbed heaven without the Lake of Fire for confinement of the wicked.

Why could not the wicked be simply blotted out? I am not God to give a total answer, but I do know from Scripture that humanity is made in the image of God. Unlike animals, human beings live on after death. It would violate the image of God for the spirit to die and cease to have consciousness even though the earthly body may be long dead and buried. Having been made in the image of God, we have everlasting existence even if that existence is in the bowels of the Lake of Fire.

Probably the most comprehensive statement of everlasting mercy and punishment is found in Revelation 21:4-8:

> *And God shall wipe away all tears from their eyes; and there shall be no more death, neither sorrow, nor crying, neither shall there be any more pain: for the former things are passed away. And He that sat upon the throne said, Behold, I make all things new. And He said unto me, Write: for these words are true and faithful. And He said unto me, It is done. I am Alpha and Omega, the Beginning and the End. I will give unto him that is athirst of the fountain of the water of life freely. He that overcomes shall inherit all things; and I will be his God, and he shall be my son. But the fearful, and unbelieving, and the abominable, and murderers, and whoremongers, and sorcerers, and idolaters, and all liars, shall have their part in the lake which burns with fire and brimstone: which is the second death.*